ARE WE LISTENING?
MAKING SENSE OF CLASSROOM BEHAVIOUR
WITH PUPILS AND PARENTS

ARE WE LISTENING?
MAKING SENSE OF CLASSROOM BEHAVIOUR WITH PUPILS AND PARENTS

Jackie Ravet

Trentham Books
Stoke on Trent, UK and Sterling, USA

Trentham Books Limited
Westview House   22883 Quicksilver Drive
734 London Road   Sterling
Oakhill   VA 20166-2012
Stoke on Trent   USA
Staffordshire
England ST4 5NP

First published 2007

British Library Cataloguing-in-Publication Data
A catalogue record for this book is available from the
British Library

ISBN-13: 978 1 85856 392 3

Cover drawing: Elio Ravet

Designed and typeset by Trentham Print Design Ltd,
Chester and printed in Great Britain by Hobbs the
Printers Ltd, Hampshire.

Want Knot

What's the biggest problem you have as a teacher?

The biggest problem?

Yeah.

Why do you ask?

Just checking my options for a career.

My biggest problem? I suppose it would be the kids who don't want to learn anything.

Don't want to learn anything?

Well, don't want to learn what I'm trying to teach.

Why is that?

Why don't they want to learn it?

No. Why is it a problem?

Because it's my job to teach them.

Your job is to teach them what they don't want to learn?

No. I think my job is to get them to want to learn it.

I see. So your job is to get them to do something they don't want to do?

Not exactly. I want them to want to learn it.

Even if they don't want to?

Yes.

Your job is to get them to want what they don't want?

Yes.

I think I'll be a plumber.

(Wilson 1991, p171)

Contents

Tables and Figures

For my parents, my husband and my children
with thanks for all you have taught me.

Acknowledgements

On the day I completed my initial teacher training, I remember very clearly emphasising to a friend of mine that whilst I was looking forward to being a class teacher, I was certain that I would not be able to handle working with pupils with what people referred to at the time as 'behaviour problems' or 'special needs'. As it turned out, most of my career has been spent teaching and researching with such pupils, and contrary to my earlier prediction, I have always found the experience immensely satisfying and hugely rewarding. Over the years, these pupils have taught me far more than I could possibly have taught them. They have forced me to think, made me reflect, stretched my practice and, frequently, required me to change. I am grateful to every one of them and could not have written this book without having had the privilege of meeting them and being their teacher.

I am also grateful to the pupils, parents and staff of Sommerville primary school (not its real name) who welcomed me into their classrooms and homes and participated in the research study that lies at the heart of this book. This research is the gem around which I have formulated the intersubjective approach to classroom disengagement explored in these pages. This approach owes much to the generous contributions and rich insights of all the Sommerville participants, and in this sense the book is as much theirs as it is mine.

However, doing research is one thing, but writing a book about it is quite another. I doubt that I would ever have considered the latter if it were not for Professor Walter Humes, who, at the time of writing, was Director of Research in the School of Education at the University of Aberdeen. It was Professor Humes who initially planted the seed for a book based on my classroom research, and without his encouragement the project would have been unthinkable. I am extremely grateful to him for seeing the potential in my work and for his enduring interest in it.

Many others have been integral to the development of the book and deserve my thanks. My editor, Gillian Klein at Trentham has, of course, been there from the beginning. I am extremely grateful for her warm support and welcome guidance over the past year. Barbara Hookey, my mentor at the University of Aberdeen, also warrants special mention as she has been a constant source of encouragement throughout the months of writing. Her unswerving faith in the book and her firm belief in its central purpose have been absolutely fundamental to me. Many other colleagues have also been supportive of the project including Leila Holm, Professor Philip Woods, Jean Kane, Allison Shoemark, Mary de Silva, Meg Taylor, Aileen Barlcay, Jane Mott and Jennifer Clarke. Several of these colleagues read sections of the book and provided valuable feedback. I am grateful to all of them.

Finally, I would like to thank my parents, my husband and my children for their enduring love and support. Special thanks must also go to my son, Elio Ravet, for the wonderful drawing that became the jacket cover for this book.

Introduction

Several years ago, before I became a lecturer and researcher, I worked as a Support for Learning Teacher in the primary sector. My work took me into many different schools and classrooms where my remit was to provide support for pupils who, for one reason or another, were struggling with various aspects of learning. As I worked in this role, I was struck by the fact that it was relatively easy to meet the needs of the majority of pupils who had a straightforward knowledge or skills gap, and who were eager to learn and happy to cooperate. It was far more difficult, however, to address the needs of the small minority of pupils who consistently found it hard to concentrate and motivate themselves, and who seemed profoundly bored by, and disinterested in, school and learning. I'm talking about pupils who were perfectly bright and capable, but who were underachieving principally because of their recurring disengagement i.e. their tendency to abandon learning in order to play, chat, wander around or daydream.

When disengaged behaviour like this becomes persistent and chronic it inevitably undermines pupil performance and has a deleterious effect on pupil achievement. However, I observed that it could also have a powerful impact on teachers. For example, it caused them significant frustration and stress, generated fears of failure and inadequacy and created tensions within the pupil/teacher relationship. Pupil behaviour and teacher response therefore seemed to become entwined in such cases, and could develop into a highly negative pattern of interaction that led to further problems all round. When parents were drawn into this negative dynamic, the problem of disengagement quickly became systemic.

It seemed to me that teachers, pupils and parents in this predicament were essentially stuck – a situation that was deeply uncomfortable for everyone. Yet, despite this stalemate, teachers knew their pupils still had to be taught. Teachers grappled with this conundrum by trying everything they could think of to re-engage them and bring them back to learning. However, when their efforts failed, which they frequently did, teachers sometimes defaulted to a strategy of low level admonishment that they hoped would make pupils relent and get them back in line. This rarely worked and tended to make a bad situation worse.

As a Support for Learning teacher I had no effective solution for this troubling problem and felt as deeply dissatisfied as the teachers around me. Our interventions with these pupils seemed to be reactive, superficial, unsystematic and, worst of all, ineffective. I was disconcerted that pupils were being coerced into conformity with teacher requirements and expectations that were rigidly held, but that had never been critically questioned. Worse, little, if any, consideration appeared to be given to how pupils and their parents perceived disengagement, how they explained the problem and where they thought the solution might lie. This failure to explore pupil and parent points of view effectively ensured that teacher perspectives were incomplete and their responses inadequate. This seemed to me to be a fundamental and serious oversight. Wasn't there a better way? Why didn't we listen to pupils?

These questions were the trigger for the research study that lies at the heart of this book. The principle aim of the book is to explore an alternative way of conceptualising pupil disengagement that is respectful, collaborative and takes pupil, teacher and parent perceptions into account. Thus, instead of dealing with disengagement by focusing largely on pupils and trying to change them, the book proceeds from the premise that a child deficit model is inappropriate and that there is no single cause of disengagement that can be 'fixed' in order to neatly resolve the problem. Rather, it is argued that the causes of disengagement are frequently multiple and diverse, and that the solutions to it are therefore likely to be varied and complex.

Facing up to this complexity rather than opting for simplistic solutions is an important strand throughout the book. Teachers are urged to embrace the idea of multiple perceptions, work jointly with pupils and parents, and seek a shared understanding of the meaning of disengagement that will put them in a far stronger position to deal with problems in the classroom. Indeed, a shared understanding will help teachers to see disengagement, not as an obstinate rejection or refusal of learning, but as a powerful and rational survival strategy that surfaces when pupils can no longer cope. Similarly, it will help them to acknowledge their own reactive and defensive interactions and see them as an understandable response to the pressures of disengagement – the teacher's way of surviving in the classroom.

Dealing with disengagement therefore requires an authentic collaboration between pupils, teachers and parents in which survival responses can be identified, addressed and replaced with more constructive and lasting forms of coping. I refer to this collaborative process as an intersubjective approach to disengagement. I hope, after reading this book, that teachers will be encouraged to consider this way of working.

1

Setting the context:
the inclusive classroom

Individuals are more complex than we can understand, and certainly more complex than allowed for by class-based teaching. (Schostack and Logan, 1984)

Every morning, after carpet time, the routine is more or less the same. On the teacher's signal, twenty-five children rise rather noisily and jostle towards their trays. After a few moments of chatting and playful nudging they collect their spelling books, jotters and pencils, and return to their places at the brightly coloured tables scattered about the room. The teacher stands with arms folded and watches the children, gently encouraging the stragglers back to their seats. Soon, heads begin to bow and the noise begins to settle as the children open their books and copy out their spellings. They are preparing for the ubiquitous Friday test.

Malcolm, as usual, is still rummaging in his tray. Pencil sharpenings, fragments of old rubber and forbidden trinkets cascade untidily to the floor. The teacher's face tightens as she catches Malcolm's eye. She says nothing but looks meaningfully at the clock. It is a familiar and well-practiced gesture intended to hurry him up and remind him of how much time matters in busy classrooms. It is enough to prompt Malcolm swiftly back to his seat, where he opens his book and picks up his pencil in what he hopes will be a convincing display of diligence.

But as the teacher relaxes and settles down to her marking, she does not see that Malcolm has abandoned his spellings and has a ruler that he is jabbing playfully into his neighbour's leg. If he is lucky, and if his neighbour is willing, this might develop into a fully-fledged sword fight under the table – just the first of many he will initiate in the long day ahead. On the other hand, there is a danger his neighbour will shoot his hand up and shout: 'He doing it again, Miss!' – just like he did yesterday. Then there'll be trouble...

Whatever happens, Malcolm will not finish his spellings. Indeed, with tiresome predictability, he will fall behind with this and many other tasks over the course of the coming weeks and months. Repeated rows, report cards and letters home will not deter him. Recklessly, he will keep going, like one of the wind up toys he sometimes sneaks into his pocket and which clatter noisily across the table in the middle of lessons. The one thing that Malcolm is clear about, and expresses frequently to anyone who will listen, is that he hates teachers and hates school. He would rather be just about anywhere else on the planet.

Malcolm's persistent disengagement has become a growing problem for his teacher, Miss James. Worryingly, he seems resistant to the usual forms of admonishment that have worked for her over three years as a primary teacher. She feels frustrated that he stubbornly ignores her repeated attempts to reach out and help him, and she senses a growing gap opening up between them. Communication is hopeless – Malcolm just doesn't seem to listen. She feels guilty that, despite her best efforts, teaching and learning have effectively come to a standstill.

Miss James knows that it might help if she could just sit down and talk to Malcolm, and give him more attention on a one-to-one basis. However, there are twenty-four other children to consider, including a child in a wheelchair who has recently joined the class. Then there are the pressures, bearing silently down on her, of assessments and attainment targets and the mountains of paper work that she never seems to get on top of. To add to this, in the background, are Malcolm's parents. They are confused and angry. They want to know what's happening, who's to blame, what can be done about it and why things never seem to change. A sequence of fraught and unsatisfactory meetings have only served to intensify matters. Mum, in particular, is unhappy with the way that Miss James is dealing with Malcolm and seems convinced that a firmer hand would get things under control. There are never any problems at home, Mum says.

Miss James tries hard not to think about the situation, but quietly inside of her grows a crushing sense of failure and a rising panic that she cannot handle things any longer. She should surely be able to reverse this pattern of disengagement and underachievement, yet she has run out of energy and feels devoid of ideas. Actually, though she finds it difficult to admit, she is at her wits end with Malcolm.

If you are a teacher you may recognise this scenario, for there are many Malcolms in many primary classrooms across the country. There are also many weary teachers who come to dread the relentless necessity to deal with disengagement on a daily basis.

The term disengagement, as it is used here, refers to a range of low-level, off-task behaviours such as joking around, chatting, daydreaming, playing and disturbing others, associated with a minority of pupils across the primary years. Whilst these behaviours might, at first glance, seem relatively trivial, research repeatedly indicates that they present a serious problem to teachers, pupils and parents (Munn *et al*, 2004). They are usually difficult to deal with, resistant to change and are associated with sustained pupil underachievement and teacher stress.

Most books on the subject refer to these behaviours as 'disruptive', disaffected' or 'troublesome' but these labels are explicitly rejected throughout this book because they imply a strong negative judgment and an *a priori* assumption that the 'problem' in question is located exclusively within the individual child. Such books tend to conceptualise behaviour that does not meet teacher expectations as a problem to be managed based on an unquestioned acceptance of teacher interpretations and judgments. These judgments generally focus on pupil deficits of personality, attitude, aptitude and ability as well as family background as the source of the 'problem behaviour'.

The term disengagement is used in preference to the labels listed above as it is purely descriptive, value-free and does not imply a problem in the child. This seems apposite in an educational context in which there is mounting concern about the validity of the child deficit model and a growing acceptance, on the basis of much educational research, that school and classroom context can influence, if not create, pupil behaviour. As a result, there has been a slow movement towards a more interactionist analysis of behaviour in the classroom informed by a social constructivist paradigm. Within this paradigm, behaviour is not simply a given – something that has a separate existence. Rather, behaviour is viewed as a construction – something inextricably linked to, and shaped by, the context in which it arises. It is also re-constructed as individuals articulate their views on the behaviour, and express their opinions and beliefs about its purpose and meaning. The aim of this book is to explore these underlying constructions in order to build up a picture of the dynamics of disengagement encapsulated in stories like Malcolm's.

A dynamic can be defined as a force that initiates, drives and energises an action and moves it forward. In this case, therefore, we are concerned with the underlying forces that drive and energise pupil disengagement. These forces are, of course, invisible. They cannot be seen, but they can be inferred. Clearly, in order to get at these forces it is necessary to look underneath surface behaviours such as those described in Malcolm's story and consider, in detail, what a specific pupil's disengagement actually means to all those most intimately involved with and affected by it – the pupils themselves, their teachers and their parents. How do they perceive the behaviours in question? How do they describe, explain and evaluate them?

This book draws on research into perceptions of disengagement to illustrate how underlying disjunctions of perception, i.e. clashes in the ways in which individuals make sense of and understand disengagement lead irrevocably to underlying distortions within the pupil, teacher and parent triangle. These distortions manifest as miscommunication, disordered interaction and skewed responses to disengagement in the classroom. These, in turn, exacerbate difficulties within the teacher/pupil relationship and perpetuate cycles of disengagement and underachievement.

The logical conclusion of this analysis is that a firm and explicit focus on the exploration and sharing of underlying subjective meanings and understandings is absolutely fundamental to the endeavour of making sense of behaviour in the primary classroom. However, this process cannot be complete unless pupil and parent perceptions are taken fully into account alongside those of teachers. Perhaps this explains why generic behaviour management strategies are so often ineffectual. They are usually imported into contexts in which teacher constructions alone predominate. They therefore operate on top of layers of underlying misunderstanding and distortion that are never exposed to the challenge of competing perspectives. This is rather akin to trying to cover up a crack in the wall by papering over the top. Eventually the cracks are bound to show through; a good reason, then, for scraping below the surface and exploring the multiple realities that lie beneath.

However, there are other reasons why this endeavour is justified, if not pressing. One of the most important is the relatively recent and dramatic shift in educational practice towards an inclusive philosophy with an emphasis on collaborative partnership with pupils and parents. Let us take a brief excursion into this territory by considering the various legislative and policy developments over the last 20 years, that have stimulated this shift. This discussion helps to illustrate how notions of teacher professionalism have evolved over recent years and why the collaborative, three-way, approach to classroom behaviour outlined in this book is now both timely and appropriate.

Inclusive practice and its implications for teacher professionalism

Up until the 1980s, teachers were generally in control of what went on in their classrooms. They could reasonably expect to shut the classroom door and get on with the task of teaching pupils more or less as they wanted. Of course, there were vague curriculum guidelines to consider, assessments to complete and other formal requirements to be taken into account. But, by and large, teachers experienced a high degree of professional autonomy. By the late 1980s however, this began to change. Two key strands of influence emerged around this time that have, over the past two decades, changed the educational landscape dramatically.

The first influence was the 1988 Education Reform Act that directly affected schools in England and Wales, and in modified form, schools throughout Scotland. This legislation was aimed directly at controlling teaching and learning in mainstream schools via curriculum reform. It was also associated with the introduction of national testing, performance indicators, league tables and the development of mechanisms for teacher regulation and accountability. Ostensibly, these measures were introduced to make it possible to measure and compare pupil learning outcomes, improve teacher performance and enhance school standards. It might also be argued that these reforms were attempts by the government of the day to promote the political ideals of control, mastery and progress by making education more scientific and objective, and by running schools rather like small businesses within a competitive market economy.

Despite pockets of deep resistance, especially in schools that might have been characterised at the time as progressive, this political agenda had the effect of restoring and consolidating a highly traditional formulation of teacher professionalism within mainstream institutions (Usher and Edwards, 1994). This formulation includes a number of important features:

- The notion of the teacher as expert in the theory and practice of teaching and learning, curriculum matters and pedagogical forms
- The notion of teacher knowledge as definitive and scientifically based

- The idea of the teacher's professional task as the transmission of a body of knowledge, belief and truth to pupils
- The belief that the processes of teaching and learning are rational, objective and dispassionate activities
- The presumption that a teacher's singular power to reshape and determine pupil behaviour is a necessary adjunct to the achievement of learning progress

This construction of the teacher is, of necessity, associated with a complementary construction of the pupil within a traditionalist framework. Thus, where the teacher is viewed as the expert, primary pupils are conceived of as individuals who, by virtue of their age, are largely unable to act as independent agents of knowledge. They are therefore perceived as being almost entirely dependent on the expert guidance of the teacher.

This notion of the pupil was justified with reference to scientific studies such as the psycho-statistical research that was conducted during the 1970s based on the early work of Jean Piaget. This body of work appeared to provide strong evidence for the innate nature of the restricted abilities and competences of the young child – their egocentricity, inflexibility of thought and limited linguistic ability (Donaldson, 1978). It also seemed to provide proof for the idea of 'developmental sequentialism' i.e. the notion that the development of thought and language in children proceeds in a linear and orderly fashion through a specific set of stages associated with maturation. Piaget's framework became the bedrock of primary education via the Plowden Report (1967).

Research therefore seemed to offer objective validation for a set of constructions that were soon transformed into prescriptive truths. Though much subsequent research has undermined the foundations of certain aspects of Paiget's work, its influence, arguably, continues to be pervasive and underpins the organisation and pedagogical form of teaching and learning in many primary classrooms today.

A restricted notion of parents as educators also reinforces and justifies traditional constructions of teacher professionalism. For example, whilst parents are construed as experts, in a highly generalised sense, both on the subject of their children as individuals and in a rather informal form of teaching and learning that takes place in the home, their knowledge and know-how is not validated in any way and has no official status (Todd and Higgins, 1998). Thus whilst parental views and opinions are superficially valued they cannot easily compete in educational debate with teachers who are regarded as the *real* experts and providers of education. Parents are therefore construed largely as consumers of education. Though changes in the political context of education in the late 1980s did much, on the surface at least, to provide opportunities for parents' participation in educational matters, the idea of participation propounded by governments and institutions was that parents should work cooperatively with agendas defined by teachers and schools and work with, not against, dominant educational ideas and leadership figures. Participation was not intended as an invitation to challenge teacher knowledge or authority, and it has not emerged in any sense as a partnership of equals (Vincent and Martin, 2005).

Teachers, according to traditional parameters, are therefore in almost total control of knowledge and truth in the classroom. Control of knowledge, it might be argued, is the foundation of power in any social context, and this is arguably the basis upon which teachers currently exercise their right, sanctioned by society, to direct and control the minds and behaviour of children. This implicit right to control is upheld and reinforced by the fact that teachers are at the top of the power hierarchy in schools. This ensures the one-way authority relationship between themselves, pupils and parents and effectively guarantees that their power base is unchallengeable.

Importantly however, teachers do not generally perceive themselves as oppressors imposing their power over pupils and parents (Vincent, 1996). On the contrary, their power is construed as entirely benign and is fully legitimised by society. To a large extent, it is also supported by pupils and parents themselves, though this support tends to be passive rather than active (*ibid*). It should also be noted that pupils and parents do not necessarily perceive themselves as an oppressed group (*ibid*) or as victims in relation to teachers, though this, of course, may sometimes be the case.

Pollard (1985) emphasises this point throughout his work on the social world of the primary classroom. His model clarifies how teachers and pupils negotiate a working consensus in the classroom, and he highlights the fact that the vast majority of pupils in primary schools accept, and indeed expect, teachers to have ultimate control. This is part of the socialisation of pupils that begins the moment they enter formal education. However, Pollard also acknowledges that there is often a small corpus of pupils in any primary classroom who will routinely reject teacher authority. The important point his that these pupils are perceived as non-conforming and exceptional – they do not, or will not, join the working consensus. Rarely, as a result of pupil non-conformity, is the consensus itself called seriously into question. Indeed, the overwhelming cultural consensus behind teacher power has, historically, ensured its invisibility and taken-for granted status. This has effectively obscured the need for any questioning of teacher power itself (Crozier and Reay, 2005).

However, the second strand of influence on education over the past two decades has upset this *status quo*. This strand can be traced back to the legislation on children's rights that began with the United Nations Convention on the Rights of the Child (1989), the Children Act (1989) and the Children (Scotland) Act (1995). These landmark pieces of legislation have developed and evolved via a raft of further acts and codes of practice in education throughout the past decade and, significantly, have become conjoined to the government drive towards inclusive education. This complex set of influences has sparked a protracted period of uncertainty and upheaval for teachers and has triggered some serious questioning of the traditional norms and values underpinning schooling and education. This has resulted in some quite remarkable developments in educational practice and a transformation in notions of teacher professionalism.

Though inclusive education is open to a range of definitions and interpretations, and is still in the early stages of implementation, it has some clear, distinguishing features. Firstly, at the heart of inclusive policy lies the requirement that practitioners teach for diversity and create classrooms in which all pupils can learn together. This includes, except in exceptional circumstances, pupils with severe and complex additional support needs. Consequently teachers in ordinary mainstream classrooms must now broaden their teaching repertoire to include curriculum and behavioural approaches and practices that have, hitherto, been the preserve of the educational specialists within specialist settings.

To add to this, teachers are no longer being asked to accept that this repertoire will be based on a scientific formulation that might provide practitioners with a clear and unambiguous recipe for teaching and learning. Rather, accumulated research now suggests that the 'how' of teaching is inextricably linked to the 'who' of learning, and it is the matching of one to the other that provides the basis for successful student progress. Indeed, it is precisely this pedagogical diversity and flexibility that teachers are currently being urged to embrace. Many teachers feel that this diversity complicates and intensifies teaching to a degree that makes it impractical and unmanageable. It obviously has considerable implications for teacher workload and stress and implies the need for significant injections of staff training and support, enhanced funding and improved resourcing, not all of which are currently forthcoming.

This shift in policy and associated shift in teacher role also means that practitioners must not just consult with fellow professionals and support agency staff, such as speech and language specialists, physiotherapists, social workers, medical professionals and so on, as they have been used to doing up until now. They must share expertise with them, problem solve with them, plan with them, and monitor and evaluate with them. In some cases they will also work alongside these professionals in the primary classroom in order to meet the diverse needs of the pupils. This represents a step beyond consultation towards a model of partnership characterised by 'deep' forms of collaboration (Head, 2003) that, potentially at least, are transformative in their outcomes for teachers and their practice and also for pupils and their learning. This model is clearly miles away from the traditional ideal of the autonomous, expert teacher.

A crucial feature of the inclusive agenda is the unprecedented emphasis placed on learner rights, especially those with additional support needs. Their entitlement to a say in decisions affecting their education and to active participation in school life is now enshrined in law. The same broad principle of inclusive involvement is also extended to parents. Educational policy therefore demands that pupil and parent contributions be actively sought and incorporated into planning for teaching and learning. This does not just mean contributions about school fund raising efforts or school uniform negotiations. It means contributions about the curriculum, target setting, individualised educational plans (IEPs) as well as behaviour. These areas have always been the traditional preserve of the classroom teacher alone, and have been assumed to require their professional expertise, knowledge and judgement. The fact that they are, potentially at least, being opened up to pupils and parents represents a considerable shift in thinking about who should be involved in educational decision making.

The findings of a large and growing body of research on pupil perspectives is complementing emerging constructions of partnership and collaboration (e.g. Flutter and Rudduck, 2004). This research has firmly indicated that, contrary to traditional assumptions, primary pupils are actually quite capable of reflecting upon their performance and behaviour in school and, given a supportive and enabling context, articulating this self-knowledge to others (*ibid*). Further, the intrinsic value of this underlying self-knowledge is becoming increasingly clear and is now understood to play a crucial role in the processes of learning and in the construction of a pupil's learning behaviour. This suggests that children, like adults, are active 'architects of action' (Cohen, 1994: 21) rather than the passive, blank slates associated with a more traditional viewpoint.

Research into pupil perspectives has therefore consolidated calls for a redefinition of traditional notions of childhood to embrace the idea of young children as active learning agents capable of constructing and reconstructing personal knowledge and deserving of a voice in matters of importance to their education (Lee, 2001). It has also stimulated the evolution of educational research methodologies appropriate to working collaboratively with children and which seek to place their perspectives at the heart of classroom investigation. As a corollary, the notion of pupil voice is beginning to gain credence in educational circles. Listening to and actively involving pupils in their education is therefore fast becoming a mainstream educational imperative and is no longer the preserve of the educational idealist.

The status now afforded parents as equal partners within the inclusive model also threatens and contradicts traditional ideals. This notion of partnership represents a significant development because it is now a requirement enshrined in law rather than an optional side show. Indeed, the recent legislation expressly promotes parents' rights to a far broader and more profound degree of influence over decisions affecting their children's education, and is quite specific about the steps parents can take if these rights are flouted. Whether parents take up these rights and powers is a different matter and the focus of some considerable debate (Crozier and Reay, 2005). Despite the legislation, many parents may well continue to take a very traditional view of their own and teachers' roles. However, the fact remains that parents have been invited into the educational arena in a way that has substantial implications for teachers. The parental influence, potentially at least, now pierces to the heart of the profession's main fortress of control – the classroom.

Taken together, all these developments clearly imply a dramatic shift away from the traditional notion of the teacher as expert and transmitter of definitive knowledge towards a more participative model of education. Implicit in this conception is an erosion of the teacher's singular power to control everything that happens in the classroom, and the introduction of the radical notion that children and parents should play a key role in teaching and learning – that they should become partners in the educational process. In this new climate of partnership with pupils and parents it is becoming more and more difficult for teachers to uphold claims to specialist knowledge and expert status, and to sustain their former position within the power hierarchy of the classroom.

As a result, some teachers complain that their work is becoming impossible and that their authority is being undermined. Others, however, argue that this new egalitarian ethos is, in principle, eminently laudable and welcome the coming of a more collaborative classroom culture with open arms. However, the situation is far from satisfactory whatever side of the fence one is on, for all teachers now find themselves in a uniquely difficult educational context in which two competing and essentially contradictory imperatives, the traditional ideal and the inclusive ideal, effectively operate side by side. Teachers must therefore negotiate a rag bag system characterised by a confusing mix of competing innovations and a plethora of opposing ideals and guidance. This poses a significant problem for the profession – how are teachers to reconcile the requirements of inclusive education within a system that is driven by competition and obsessed with standards and attainment? This confusion of policy and practice is hitting the profession hard and is generating a great deal of resentment and resistance.

These conflicts and tensions have inevitably had an impact on conceptions of behaviour and discipline within educational discourse. For example, traditional discourse tends to attribute behavioural problems in schools to a breakdown in discipline in the home, with a particular focus on pupils from single parent families, working class backgrounds, ethnic minorities and inner city communities (Araujo, 2005). Teachers are generally constructed as the victims within this discourse, and are required to use their expertise to ameliorate the worst effects of indiscipline by managing misbehaviour and changing pupil responses in the classroom. A deficit model of communities, parents and pupils is often implicit here (*ibid*) and is associated with calls for the strengthening of teacher powers to intervene and, if necessary, exclude pupils perceived as having behavioural problems.

However, it is difficult to see how this reassertion of teacher power and control is compatible with an inclusive philosophy that champions pupil and parent points of view and rights to participation. Indeed, confusingly, and running concurrently alongside this discourse, is the idea that schools should become more aware of the ways educational contexts might directly influence, and in some cases, produce disengagement. The Elton Report on *Discipline In Schools* (DES, 1989) in England and Wales, and the Scottish HMI report *Choosing With Care* (HMSO, 1990) might both be viewed as landmark documents in this sphere. Both express concern at the predominance of explanations of pupil behaviour based on social and psychological deficit models and the associated assumption that pupil behaviour is beyond the reach and responsibility of teachers.

A growing body of evidence from school effectiveness researchers suggests that teachers and the classroom environment actually have a significant influence on pupil behaviour (Reynolds and Cuttance, 1992). This research has strengthened the argument for the involvement of pupils in matters of discipline, and has highlighted the benefits to be gained from talking to disengaging pupils about their perceptions of their learning, behaviour, teachers and schools. This development clearly sits more comfortably within the inclusive ethos currently emerging within education. Indeed, it is strongly reflected in current educational policy on behaviour (SEED, 2001; DfES, 2003b) that emphasises partnerships with pupils and highlights the role of a positive, supportive ethos in preventing and responding to indiscipline in schools.

However, Hargreaves (1994) was quick to highlight the dangers, for teachers, of this complex mix of competing agendas. He warns that teachers are increasingly confronted by the 'need for more relevant and engaging student learning, for more continuous and connected professional development, and for more flexible and inclusive decision-making' (p28). Yet he acknowledges the continuing and deeply entrenched allure of a more traditional view of teaching, learning and education. Many influences within the culture still favour this view and argue passionately for the reconsolidation of teacher authority in the face of the contradictions and tensions set out above. Indeed, these are used to justify an about turn.

However, Hargreaves predicts that a reactionary response such as this would simply sharpen the crisis for schools and teachers. He warns that it could fuel a power struggle between pupils, teachers and parents that would result in more, not less, classroom chaos. He therefore argues forcefully for educational restructuring and emphasises that there is a need for a new vision of education which can reconcile conflicting influences, accommodate multiple realities, and reconcile notions of teacher power with those of pupil agency, voice and participation. He states:

> A world of voice without vision is a world reduced to chaotic babble where there are no means for arbitrating between voices, reconciling them or drawing them together. This is the dark side of the late-modern world, a world from which community and authority have disappeared. It is a world where

the authority of voice has supplanted the voice of authority to an excessive degree... A major challenge for educational restructuring is to work through and reconcile this tension between vision and voice; to create a choir from a cacophony. (Hargreaves, 1994: 251)

Towards a new vision

There is a way forward. The purpose of this book is to explore the possibility of a participatory approach to disengagement in the primary classroom that might encompass teacher, pupil and parent perspectives, and enable teachers, in a small but significant way, to begin the process of 'creating a choir from a cacophony' within the primary classroom. This is referred to as an intersubjective approach to disengagement because its focus, literally, is upon enhancing the quality of the relationship and communication between – inter – individuals – subjects – by clarifying and synthesising their personal points of view.

In the chapters that follow, I draw on the research to illustrate the significance of subjective perceptions for our understanding of pupil disengagement. This discussion explores why partnership with pupils and parents offers a route to greater social justice and inclusion in our schools, and considers how this might be done, in practical terms, in relation to behavioural issues within the primary classroom.

In chapter two, I pick up many of the issues raised above. The theory of interactionism is introduced, and its relevance is highlighted with close reference to a research study of teacher, pupil and parent perceptions of disengagement. This is referred to as the Sommerville study. This discussion clarifies the reasons why there is a case for a detailed micro-analysis of what, exactly, is happening in classrooms when learning behaviour breaks down.

Chapters three, four and five take a detailed look at the implications of the Sommerville study with a focus on pupils in chapter three, then on teachers and parents in the next two. This trio of chapters teases out the underlying purposes of pupil disengagement, and the underlying purposes of teacher and parent responses to it. Links are made to the wider research in the field in order to place the discussion within a broader context. A model of disengagement and intervention is also developed that draws the principle findings of the Sommerville study together.

Chapter six presents a practical, intersubjective model of teacher, pupil and parent partnership that might provide a more effective, inclusive response to disengagement in the classroom. The notion of the reflective practitioner plays a pivotal role within this model and is applied, using a case study format, to illustrate how the intersubjective approach might operate.

In the final chapter, the key issues and themes raised in the book are further developed. In particular, the chapter foreshadows the resistance to deep change that is the likely response of many practitioners and educationists. Barriers to intersubjectivity are therefore explored, including the cultural, political, institutional and biographical factors that can make it difficult for teachers to truly listen to pupils and embrace competing points of view. Barriers to genuine pupil and parent participation are also considered.

Nonetheless, the profession is challenged to take up the banner of collaborative practice by daring to drop their expert roles; daring to question dominant discourses on behaviour; daring to share power; and by daring to engage with the creative and practical task of creating classrooms that are consistent with the values of a democratic, inclusive philosophy, in which teacher, pupil and parent voices can all be heard.

***

Remember Malcolm?

This book has been written with the voices of children and parents still fresh in my ears: those I have taught and come into contact with as a practitioner, and those I worked closely with as a researcher. These voices are not the cacophony that Hargreaves warns us of. On the contrary, they cry out, albeit in different ways and for different reasons, for the right to be heard, to be accepted, to be a real part of things and to make a difference of some sort. These voices tell us that children and parents always feel dignified and empowered by the simple act of being taken seriously.

The voices of teachers also ring through these pages. The vast majority have the instinct to reach out and connect with pupils and parents, and know instinctively what a difference this will make to everything they do as professionals. However, they feel restricted and constrained by time, conflicting expectations, workload and a myriad of other pressures from within and without the classroom, and feel forced to hunker down and jump through the many hoops set before them. This skimming along the surface of the job robs them of satisfaction and frustrates their desire to be the teachers they know they can be.

Teachers, therefore, need to be heard too. They say they want to be human in the classroom and to create learning communities that are warm, responsive, nurturing and fun. They are willing to take risks and experiment wherever they are given the permission and support to do so. I hope that the message of this book is that such things are possible and that the idea of teachers, pupils and parents working together in partnership is not some impossibly naïve dream, but a realisable, do-able and, above all, rewarding way for everyone to learn – in the broadest sense of the term.

2

The view from nowhere

It is the perception, not the reality, which is crucial in determining behaviour. (Carl Rogers, 1969)

Imagine, for a moment, that you were the teacher witnessing Malcolm's ruler fight under the table described in chapter one. What thoughts and feelings would you have, and what action would you take as a result?

Some of you might feel irritated by the audacity of Malcolm's behaviour, and would wish to admonish him promptly and devise a suitable punishment to discourage any repetition of the incident. Alternatively, you might react with feelings of guilt and a sense of responsibility for Malcolm's lack of attention. This might be associated with a conviction that the best way forward would be to find a means of motivating Malcolm so that he would be more inclined to engage appropriately in the future. Another, quite different response, would be to perceive his behaviour as attention seeking. In this case, you might deliberately withhold any reaction to avoid reinforcing the inappropriate behaviour and respond, instead, with a programme of rewards to encourage more desirable responses.

There will be any number of variations and combinations of the above, depending upon who you are and how you have processed and interpreted the drama of the ruler fight. Imagine, however, how this variety would expand if we consider how a parent might have viewed the scenario. Then add to this how Malcolm himself might have perceived it.

By now you will see the point I am trying to make: that teachers, pupils, parents – all of us – are inevitably subject to, and are to varying degrees driven by, subjective perceptions that shape our responses and actions. Given this diversity, it seems clear that a teacher's point of view is only one amongst many and will not necessarily reflect the point of view of others. Should we not, therefore, question the validity of teacher judgements, decisions and interventions in relation to pupil behaviour that have been developed without any consultation with pupils and parents?

When the question is expressed in this way, the answer may seem perfectly obvious. However, the matter is not as straightforward as it seems for, in everyday life, we frequently lose our grip on the complexity described above. As teachers, we act *as though* our own perceptions are the only ones that exist and matter, and we act upon them as though they must be right or true. Arguably, most of the time, this may not be of any great significance. However, in the context of persistent disengagement, where teacher responses have a direct bearing on the quality of a pupil's experience in the classroom, and can result in regular admonishment, punishment and, in the worst cases, exclusion, this is surely of some considerable import.

We therefore explore the matter of perceptions in a little more detail in order to clarify what they are, how they develop and why they are of direct relevance to this analysis of disengagement. The theory of interactionism is then introduced. This discussion sets the scene for an examination of some examples of perceptions of disengagement later on in the chapter.

What are perceptions?

The discussion above raised the possibility that there is a 'common delusion' about life to which many of us subscribe without ever reflecting upon it i.e. the delusion that there is a singular reality or truth about ourselves, others and events in the world around us that we can readily trust and rely upon and that everyone shares (Wilson, 1991, p2). Superficially, our sense of reality seems immediate and unproblematic. Indeed, this accounts for the way that our perceptions seduce and capture us, and foster within us a robust belief in their value and validity.

However, a deeper understanding of the workings of the mind reveals that our sense of reality is actually based upon a highly complex, contingent and subjective set of inner processes that are constantly at work interpreting and re-interpreting incoming sensory stimuli (Bruner, 1996). Our perceptions might therefore be defined as the range of personal beliefs and opinions that are the product of this interpretive process – our informal theories about ourselves and the world (*ibid*). Perceptions are not, therefore, a direct reflection of an objective reality. They are the outcome of the highly individualised way the human mind mediates and constructs reality.

One way of testing this idea for ourselves is to consciously listen-in to the interior dialogue we continually have with ourselves right at the back of our minds – our 'self-talk'. Self-talk is an unremitting inner commentary on all that we do and experience during our waking hours, and is so ubiquitous and taken for granted that, generally speaking, we barely register its existence at all. We are easily inured by its familiarity.

This self-talk provides a small window through which the contents of our underlying perceptions might be glimpsed. Indeed, paying attention to self-talk allows us to listen-in to the way we continually chew over reality as we try to make sense of the myriad of incoming stimuli that assail us.

However, if we step back quietly, and listen critically, we will notice that our self-talk is often laden with assumptions, biases, judgments and exaggerations that can be highly robust and cause considerable rigidity in our thinking. Sometimes, self-talk can also be contradictory. Today we are telling ourselves one thing; tomorrow it's the opposite. Yet, unless we are very self-aware and deliberate in our thought and action, this self-talk can exert a powerful underlying hold on us that is externalised as knee-jerk reactions and ill-considered behaviour. Our perceptions, then, can be fickle friends. They are not always the wise and reliable font of truth and knowledge we might wish them to be. Indeed, at times, for all of us, they may amount to *mis*interpretations and illusions of reality – or what we call reality.

How do they come about?

Interactionism and the development of perceptions

Perceptions have been defined as our interpretations of incoming sensory stimuli – our theories about reality. Social constructivists argue that these interpretations are shaped by a number of complex and interacting layers of influence. At the micro level, they are informed by our nature i.e. our genetic make-up and resulting biological propensities and potentialities. They are also deeply enmeshed in our experiences with those closest to us, especially those who nurtured us and influenced us during our earliest years of growth and development. Indeed, the behaviour, attitudes, values and beliefs of parents, siblings, peers and other significant people in our lives generally make a profound impression on us and are an important shaping influence on the way we think and behave. We must add to this the influence of the wider social network in which we live and grow, including our experiences and interactions within our community, school and workplace.

At the macro level, perceptions are further shaped by cultural constructions, ideas and norms communicated via books, television, radio, computers and other influential media. These sources transmit the specific sets of understandings about life and living relevant to the historical time, place and cultural context we find ourselves in, and constitute the broader social reality we occupy. So it is highly relevant, in terms of the study of perceptions, whether we were born in 1990 or in 1960; whether we come from Scotland or from India; and whether we live in a caravan or in a palace. All these factors contribute to our sense of who we are and to the sorts of perceptions we have of the world.

However, we are not passively determined by these influences as if we were empty vessels. Rather, the process is an interactive one – a joint enterprise between the individual and the environment. For example, when we meet others during social interaction, we are constantly in the process of interpreting their language, gestures and responses i.e. their symbols of communication. This interaction provides us with information about others and the world that is immediately filtered through the interpretive system i.e. checked and balanced against feedback from others sources and contexts and then slotted into the jigsaw of perceptions carried within.

Social interaction also provides us with information about ourselves as we are seen through the eyes of others. This is known as the 'looking glass' effect of interaction (Cooley, 1902). Reflections glimpsed through this looking glass are filtered and processed in a similar fashion, forming the warp and weft of our sense of self. But our perceptions at any one moment are not cast in stone. On the contrary, they are subject to constant re-evaluation and reconstruction on the basis of future stimuli. The whole process is like an internal story that is continually being developed, edited, revised and updated.

This metaphor of the story is entirely apposite when we consider the human tendency to narrativise experience during everyday conversation (Bruner, 1990). Again, if we stand back and listen-in to ourselves as we speak to others we will hear the stories we tell about ourselves. They can be deeply illuminating and sometimes surprising. This story-telling is another dimension of the interpretive process. It is a mechanism that enables us to explore and rehearse our meanings and understandings and express them to ourselves whilst we are expressing them to others. These stories draw together and encode our 'truth' as it stands at any particular moment, unifying whatever knowledge, beliefs, insights, biases and delusions we may harbour on any specific theme. They are a powerful expression of our subjective truth.

Our sense of internal and external reality is therefore mediated by an inter-actional process that involves ongoing assimilation, adaptation and change over time. This process, as we have discovered, depends on the rich fabric of our personal experiences. It also depends on other important factors such as our level of awareness and self-awareness, our affective and cognitive development and the way our subjective impressions are organised and ordered. The interpretive process is therefore a complex, highly indivi-dualised and active function that mediates the passage of external stimuli. It explains the uniqueness of our sense of self and reality, and the highly sub-jective quality of our perceptions.

Yet we must remember that because individuals in social contexts generally share a common language and participate, to a greater or lesser degree, in shared cultural experiences and a cultural consensus about the nature of the world, one's understanding of reality is never wholly subjective. We are not, in this sense, islands entirely unto ourselves. Rather, we are 'intersubjective' be-ings. Indeed, it is this intersubjectivity that enables us to communicate and understand one another most of the time, and which facilitates our pleasure in social interaction.

Many of our fundamental perceptions of reality are therefore shared. How-ever, this is more likely to happen when we are amongst those within our own culture, and is even more likely when we are amongst those within our own specific family unit and social grouping. Conversely, it is more difficult to achieve a shared sense of reality in a context that is culturally and socially diverse and where a multiplicity of realities struggle to co-exist. The primary classroom is a prime example of such a context.

Bruner (1990) therefore stresses that any study of people's perceptions can only be approached from the inside, by focusing on both the socio-cultural and historical context in which they arise and the individual's perceptions of self as they are applied within the immediate context. He argues forcefully that any attempt to understand people's behaviour objectively, by watching from the outside, simply cannot be achieved. He calls this 'the view from no-where' (*ibid*, p14) – hence the title of this chapter. Is this not the view from which most teachers attempt to understand pupil behaviour? Perhaps this explains their ongoing frustration and stress, and their feeling that they never really get to the bottom of the problem.

What matters, therefore, is not only what people do, but what they think they are doing; not just what happens, but how experiences and events are subjec-tively interpreted. The Carl Rogers quote that opens this chapter encapsulates this idea perfectly. So if we wish to determine the meaning of pupil behaviour in the classroom, avoiding the 'view from nowhere', it is vital to consider pupil self-perceptions. These perceptions can help teachers to understand underlying pupil motivations and purposes, and will enable them to make more accurate and informed decisions about pupil needs and support.

Let us now take a look at a research study that provides some lived examples of contrasting perceptions. These examples illustrate and illuminate the discussion we have had so far and will soon clarify why teachers, relying solely upon their own unchallenged perceptions, are generally ill equipped to make sense of, and deal with, the disengagement that confronts them. This book argues that the attempt to manage pupil behaviour on this basis is likely to be damaging for teachers and pupils alike.

Making sense of pupil, teacher and parent perceptions: the Sommerville study

Sommerville primary is the name I have given, to protect its identity, to a school in a small town in northeast Scotland. It was here that I conducted a research study of pupil, teacher and parent perceptions of disengagement. All the pupils in the research group were eight or nine years of age and were drawn from mixed ability classes of between twenty and twenty-five pupils. The research cohort included ten pupils – nine boys and one girl. This gender imbalance is fairly typical in the area of pupil disengagement (Munn *et al*, 2004).

Five teachers participated in the research and they initially identified potential pupil participants whom they perceived as disengagers – pupils who persistently resist, reject or refuse formal learning tasks as a result of regular off-task behaviours such as chatting, walking around, daydreaming, playing, fighting, joking about etc. (Pupils with a record of need were excluded from the study.) These behaviours were responsible for a pattern of chronic underachievement amongst all the pupils under consideration. They were also a source of frustration and stress for the teachers involved.

The parents of the ten pupils were also invited to participate in the study. They were included because it was anticipated that they might provide a contrasting set of perceptions implicitly informed by their detailed biographical knowledge of their child, their understanding of the historical and socio-cultural influences upon them, and an awareness of their child's behaviour in contexts beyond the classroom. Thus parents would be able to make sense of pupil behaviour within a far broader context than could ever be possible for teachers.

Importantly, the parents in the study were not in the classroom to witness their child's disengagement directly. Their perceptions were therefore based not on what they had seen but on what they had heard about the behaviour from their children, from teachers and other sources, and on their intimate knowledge of their child and general understanding of their behaviour.

Purpose

The central purpose of the Sommerville study was to establish the meaning of the recurring disengaged behaviour of each of the ten pupils from the point of view of teachers, parents and the pupils themselves. Three specific questions guided the investigation:

- How do disengaging pupils perceive themselves as learners in the classroom i.e. how do they describe, explain and evaluate their disengaged behaviour?
- How do teachers and parents describe, explain and evaluate their behaviours, and how do their perceptions compare with those of the pupils?
- What can the study of pupil, teacher and parent perceptions contribute to the endeavour of making sense of pupil behaviour in learning contexts?

Before we consider the findings of the study it is important to have a brief discussion of the way the study was conducted – its methodology – so that readers can gain some idea of how pupil, teacher and parent perceptions were gathered and analysed.

This is important because the various methods researchers use in educational settings have a direct influence upon the sort of data they generate, the quality of this data and therefore the trustworthiness of the findings. The discussion is also important because the study of perceptions is by no means a straightforward matter, especially where primary aged pupils are concerned. Some exploration of methodology in therefore in order.

Interpretative methods

The study of pupil, teacher and parent perceptions was approached using what is known as an interpretative methodology. The following summary sets out some of the key characteristics of this approach, giving the reader an idea of what the term implies within the context of the research under consideration:

- the collection of data in natural settings e.g. schools and classrooms, rather than in clinical settings e.g. laboratories or other settings that have been artificially created

- the immersion of the researcher within the research context along-side participants over a long term period – in this case one academic year

- the avoidance of methods of data collection that might artificially organise and distort subjective meanings (e.g. questionnaires) and a preference for the use of observations and open-ended interviews

- the deliberate cultivation, on behalf of the researcher, of a critical, reflective orientation to all that is seen, said and done in the research context in order to minimise distortions arising from researcher bias

The practices and approaches designed to enable the participation of the ten pupils in the cohort also require mention here. The involvement of young children in research introduces a subtle complexity into the process because of their age and inexperience and also their vulnerability to the power of adults. Young pupils must therefore be explicitly supported or enabled to participate in research studies so that their capacity for contributing is maximised and to ensure that adult influence and interference is minimised, especially the influences arising from asymmetries of power.

Pupil interviews were therefore planned as activity based formats rather than the straightforward face-to-face interviews organised for parents and teachers. The activities were designed so that pupils could easily draw on their abilities and interests. Thus story formats, picture stimuli, drawing activities and video extracts were all used as a basis for pupil interviews. It was felt that this wide variety of modes of presentation would have a number of benefits such as enhancing motivation, concretising complex and abstract ideas, scaffolding pupil responses and also meeting individual needs in respect of pupils' varying cognitive and linguistic styles and abilities (Cooper, 1993a). Thus pupils who were less inclined to articulate their perceptions verbally had the opportunity to express themselves visually if this seemed to help them.

Further adaptive measures were also taken in view of the age of the pupils. For example, allowance was made for the fact that some young pupils tend to give simple yes/no answers rather than elaborated responses to adult questions. They may also try to anticipate a 'right' answer. The pupils were therefore explicitly assured that there was no single correct answer to researcher questions and that the researcher did not have any answers either. This was supported by the inversion of the expert status of the researcher from the outset of the study when it was clarified that the researcher and pupil participants would be working together on a joint venture throughout the research, and not in customary teacher/pupil roles. Elaboration and depth of pupil response was facilitated by keeping pupil questions as open-ended as possible, and by drawing extensively on pupils' lived experience of disengagement rather than discussing the matter in the abstract (Van Manen, 1997).

Some researchers (e.g. Cooper, 1993b) suggest that it is important to try to ensure that pupil responses are authentic rather than merely reconstructions of adult views – the views of parents and teachers, perhaps, or even the view the pupil thinks the researcher wishes to hear. However, the quest for authenticity is actually highly problematic and centres upon the difficulty of reliably distinguishing authentic responses from inauthentic. How is the researcher to tell these apart? Thus, whilst careful attention was paid to the avoidance of leading questions and the dangers of talking *for* pupils rather than *with* them (Fielding, 2004), it was the premise of this study that perceptions, be they adult or child, should be taken at face value.

Having said this, every effort was made to broaden, deepen and consolidate pupil responses via a research design that enabled them to visit their perceptions of their disengagement again and again from various different angles using different modes of expression and communication. The data analysis focused largely on the responses that recurred over time and proved themselves to be robustly representative of the views of the individual. Nonetheless, inconsistencies and self-contradictions can be illuminating, so these were also noted and included in the research findings.

What mattered, essentially, was that pupils find their own voice. In order to facilitate this, it was vital that pupils felt safe and well supported. The creation of a warm, accepting relationship between researcher and pupils was obviously crucial in this respect. The development of a positive and enabling context for interaction was also important.

An explicit ethical framework is always used in research with children in order to ensure respectful practices and procedures (Lindsay, 2000). Thus, pupil participants, like teachers and parents, were invited to join the study only after a full briefing as to its aims, purpose and likely outcomes. They were assured that they could leave the study at any point, and that their contributions would not, under any circumstances, be shared with their teachers or parents. Full confidentiality and anonymity therefore applied to the pupils as well as to the adults in the study.

As a final note, it ought to be stressed that the findings of the Sommerville study presented below are not offered as a set of truths about the pupils, teachers and parents who took part in the research. Naturally, their perceptions are only representative of the particular moment and specific context of the study, and these are likely to change and move on over time. Their accounts have also been subject to systematic interpretation and analysis and must, ultimately, be understood as researcher constructions. Having said this, every effort was made to ensure that these accounts remained true to their original meanings, and faithful to their original spirit. Thus, *in-vivo* terms and participant utterances are quoted frequently throughout the presentation to follow.

The findings are also based on a very small sample of participants so are not offered as scientific generalisations that can be directly applied to other pupils, teachers and parents. Interpretive research does not seek to generate claims of this nature as they are fundamentally incompatible with a social constructivist theory of knowledge. Rather, the findings may have value as 'naturalistic generalisations' that might be 'intuitively' related to other contexts and validated through practice (Elliott, 1985 in Somekh, 2006, p28). Thus, teachers and student teachers reading this book may well find that they can relate much of what they read directly to their own experience of pupils, teachers, parents and primary classrooms. However, as we shall see in chapter three, four and five, the findings are corroborated by many other research studies within the field.

Perceptions of disengagement: the findings of the Sommerville study

Not surprisingly, all the participants in the Sommerville study had highly individualised views of pupil disengagement. Their accounts revealed their subjective descriptions of, explanations for and evaluations of pupil behaviour, and the idiosyncratic labels and modes of expression they used to articulate them. All participants therefore had what might be termed a unique and personal 'field of perception' i.e. a clearly bounded and personal array of views and opinions on pupil behaviour predicated upon their underlying subjective experiences, beliefs, assumptions, and meanings and delimited by the various errors, biases, illusions and misunderstandings that inevitably constrain an individual's perceptions (Goleman, 1996).

However, a comparative analysis of pupil, teacher and parent accounts un-covered the many commonalities and disparities of perception that occurred across all these individual fields. These commonalities and disparities were also a key concern of the research study and facilitated the development of three 'group' fields of perception: the pupil, teacher and parent group fields. What did the participants in each group agree and disagree on, and how did perceptions converge or diverge across the three fields?

For the purposes of this discussion I answer this question with reference to the findings in three key areas that emerged from the research data:

- Perceptions of surface behaviour
- Perceptions of pupil feeling state
- Explanations for pupil disengagement

1. Perceptions of surface behaviour

As pupils, teachers and parents talked about their perceptions of disengage-ment in the primary classroom, it became clear that their descriptions of pupil behaviour (i.e. the surface acts they observed in the classroom) showed a particular pattern of commonality and divergence.

The main finding was that teacher and parent perceptions of surface be-haviour converged much more frequently than teacher/pupil and parent/pupil perceptions. Two insights immediately flow from this. Firstly, since the parents in the study did not directly witness pupil disengagement in the classroom for themselves, it implies that their perceptions may have been more influenced by teacher perspectives passed on through formal and infor-mal reports, conversations and parent evenings, than by the self-perceptions of their children. It also tells us that the three key players in the study did not necessarily agree upon the fundamental matter at the heart of the inquiry – the nature of the specific behaviours that characterise a pupil's disengage-ment. An example will help to illustrate this finding.

Michael and his mother, Mrs Dobson, both reported that he tends to 'chat, play and take time out' from learning in the classroom by distracting himself in various ways. Michael explained that he really enjoys chatting and tries to create opportunities for doing so by making bogus trips to the wastepaper basket with his pencil sharpener so he can socialise with friends *en route*! Playing with rubbers and school equipment was another favoured pastime he reported, and he also confessed that frequent trips to the toilet gave him 'a wee rest off work.' Mrs Dobson agreed that Michael 'gets carried away' chat-ting and playing with peers in the classroom and is 'very easily distracted'.

However, Michael's teacher, Mrs Reid, did not mention any of these social behaviours when she reflected upon Michael's behaviour in the classroom. Instead, her perceptions focused upon the fact that he is 'apathetic' and 'generally slow in everything he does' especially as regards the mechanical task of writing. She also commented that Michael 'seems to spend his life daydreaming'.

Michael's mother also mentioned that he could be a dreamer and had poor concentration. She agreed that her son is 'slow getting things written down'. She said: 'Getting him to write anything down is a hassle. He'll do it, but in his own time.' So there was clearly some commonality of perception between parent and teacher in this case. Yet Michael himself did not mention any of these behaviours.

This example illustrates that it cannot be taken for granted that pupils, teachers and parents perceive disengagement in the classroom in a uniform way. Thus, behaviours that are significant to teachers and parents may be invisible to pupils, and vice versa. I use the word invisible advisedly here, meaning a metaphorical blindness to certain behaviours. Michael, for example, appears to be blind to his slowness, and his teacher, Mrs Reid, is blind to his social life in the classroom. Mrs Dobson, on the other hand, perceives and acknowledges both these sets of behaviours.

These zones of invisibility might be labelled perception gaps – a term that connotes a lack of perceptual awareness of specific acts, situations and events, whether the gap arises consciously through the deliberate rejection or suppression of specific behaviours from awareness, or is the result of unconscious processes. The concept of perceptions gaps will be one that we return to and explore in chapter four.

The findings in the area of perceptions of surface behaviour also highlighted the differing ways in which teachers, pupils and parents label what they see. Teachers and parents, for example, tended to apply a number of recurring and rather negative labels, referring to disengaged acts as 'attention seeking', 'disruptive' and 'distracted' behaviours. Teachers also used professional terms such as 'delaying tactics' and 'avoidance strategies' which parents and pupils did not employ. Pupils, by contrast, generally used more descriptive, neutral or positive labels such as 'daydreaming', 'having fun', 'having a laugh', and 'doing nothing'.

These language differentials (Somekh, 1994) are interesting because they betray underlying values and judgments and tell us a great deal about the attitude of participants towards the behaviour in question. It seems clear that pupil labels reflect a rather more positive set of evaluations and judgments than teacher and parent labels. Further, teacher and parent labels seem to assume a direct link to work avoidance or an intention to disrupt.

2. Perceptions of pupil feeling state

Feelings emerged as an important theme across participant perceptions of disengagement. However, the pupils and parents in the study were far more likely than teachers to refer to feelings, though parents did not necessarily attribute exactly the same feeling states as their children.

The commonalities between parents and pupils in this area may, at least in part, be linked to the process of mediation mentioned above. For example, it is not difficult to imagine that pupils might be far more willing to share their feelings with parents than with teachers. Parents might also be in a stronger position to pick up their children's feelings, even those that are not directly articulated. However, feeling states can often be determined by body language, facial expression and other non-verbal means. So a lack of direct communication with pupils does not wholly explain why the teachers in this cohort seemed to have so little grasp of pupil feelings in the classroom.

Pupils referred again and again to feelings associated with their learning that ranged through hatred, anger, fear, fatigue and boredom. Seven out of the ten pupils in the study directly associated feelings of boredom with the formal curriculum – especially writing and maths. However, half the pupils also mentioned feelings of fun and enjoyment that they linked directly to their acts of disengagement. A few also associated these positive feelings with active learning experiences and the more informal areas of the curriculum such as PE and music.

Hannah, her teacher Mrs Mitchell, and her mother Mrs Young, were all in full agreement that she is a pupil who frequently feels upset and angry in the classroom. Hannah stated categorically that she 'hates' her teacher and she harboured a fantasy she referred to frequently, of packing her bags and marching out the classroom the next time she was told off. This fantasy never became a reality.

Mrs Young's report confirmed these perceptions. She commented that her daughter is 'easily upset' when she is reprimanded by her teacher. She suggested that Hannah's feelings are so powerful that she regularly 'calls a sickie' in order to stay off school.

Mrs Mitchell, Hannah's teacher, also seemed to be aware of her strong feelings towards her, and suggested that they might result from a sense of rejection. She stated: 'I think that Hannah would possibly perceive that just because I try to keep on top of [things] all the time, she possibly sees it that, you know, I don't like her. But that's not the case.' Negative feelings of upset and anger aroused by the teacher seem to be a common thread in the perceptions of pupil, teacher and parent in this case.

However, Hannah disclosed other feeling states that her teacher and mother did not perceive at all. For example, she revealed that though she generally dislikes school, she does 'have fun' in the classroom when she is disengaged from learning. For example, fun is generated when she plays, talks and laughs with friends, particularly her friend Simon. This tends to happen when she is 'bored with work', especially language work and maths. But Hannah 'hates' most of the other learning activities in the classroom except P.E, music, sewing and swimming.

Mrs Mitchell and Mrs Young appeared to be unaware of Hannah's boredom with much of the school curriculum, and did not perceive how much fun and enjoyment she experienced when disengaging. This example highlights their specific perceptions gaps in relation to Hannah's feeling state, and illustrates the selective and fragmented nature of their perceptions of her.

However, one teacher, Mrs Parker, stood out as an exception in the teacher cohort. She appeared to make explicit and active attempts to discover and enhance the emotional well-being of the disengaging pupils in her class by specifically involving them in discussions about their feelings and perceptions. She collaborated with them in joint problem-solving activities that enabled them to identify and confront their difficulties. She also involved them in the design of strategies for self-monitoring, self-improvement, and self-assessment. Crucially, she sought to build warm, trusting and respectful relationships with her pupils in order to create a safe and reliable context in which this joint endeavour could flourish. It may be significant that Mrs Parker's three pupils were the only ones in the cohort who made progress across the research period in terms of reduced disengagement and improved academic achievement – a judgement corroborated by the pupils themselves and their parents.

Mrs Parker's perceptions of her pupils were therefore qualitatively different to the perceptions of the other teachers in the cohort in that they were informed, to some degree, by pupil points of view. Her responses to their behaviour were quite distinct as a result. In chapter four we look more closely at

Mrs Parker's case and her highly idiosyncratic approach to disengagement. Her practice provides some useful clues as to the sorts of collaborative strategies that can play a key role in the development of a practical and manageable approach to disengagement.

3. Explanations for pupil disengagement

Pupil, teacher and parent explanations for disengagement refer to the distinctive ways in which participants attributed causes or origins to pupil behaviour. This was an area of considerable perceptual divergence amongst the research participants in the study, and was suggestive of a distinct lack of intersubjectivity, or shared understanding, about why disengagement arises in the classroom.

Pupil explanations

Overall, pupil explanations for their disengaged behaviour had little in common with either teacher or parent explanations. Pupil explanations covered a wide range of factors, twelve in total, and fell into two broad categories. One category, labelled 'context factors', included all those explanations associated with the immediate context of the classroom and the educational and social experiences that take place in classrooms e.g. explanations linked to the curriculum and to relationships with teachers and peers. The other category was labelled 'self' factors i.e. those that were associated with personal and biographical influences. This category included the behaviours that pupils identified as being habitual and irresistible in some way, together with fatigue, laziness and 'forgetting to be good'. Pupil perceptions in these two categories are set out in Table 1 on page 32.

This table indicates that from the wide array of explanations expressed by pupils, those associated with problems with the curriculum are the most numerous. 'Boredom' with the curriculum is quite clearly the most common explanation given by pupils for their disengagement, as examples illustrate.

Michael and Gary complained bitterly that they were bored with the curriculum in general. Michael said: 'I don't like doing my work ... it's boring'. He explained that this was because 'there's too much maths' and too little of the sort of activities he enjoys like 'getting outside' and 'making things'. Michael found that disengaging by socialising with friends, sharpening pencils or going to the toilet relieved his boredom.

Likewise, Gary admitted that he got bored because he 'doesn't really enjoy most of the stuff'. Hannah also stated categorically: 'I'm bored with work ...

Table 1: Pupil explanations

Number of pupils Explanations

	Context Factors:
7	Boredom (with curriculum)
4	Volume and pace of work
3	Cognitive saturation
3	Relationships with teachers
3	Relationships with peers
1	Lack of fun
1	Difficulty of work
1	Problems generating ideas
	Self Factors:
4	Compulsive behaviours e.g chatting, daydreaming, etc
4	Fatigue
1	Laziness
1	Forgetting to be good

because it tires you out ... I'd rather play all day'. Simon explained that he frequently got bored with writing tasks. His solution was to simply put them away in his folder in order to 'do something else'. Ian expressed similar feelings about writing, and stated that he got bored because '...[writing] just takes too long. You have to concentrate too hard'. When he got bored in this way he stopped work, downed tools, and would 'sit around' and 'have a rest'.

Andrew's boredom was also associated with particular learning tasks. He recalled: '...the last time I was bored I was doing clock maths, and I hate clock maths, and I was going like this (mimes 'boredom') and not wanting to do clocks and just sitting there...'. Frank explained that his boredom sets in when a learning problem is taxing his mind, causing cognitive confusion. At this point Frank found that he would 'just start getting bored and not know what to do'. His solution was to sit quietly and daydream.

Thus for some pupils, boredom appeared linked to a general dislike of and disinterest in the curriculum or a dislike of specific sorts of learning activity such as writing tasks. For other pupils, boredom was linked not so much with the content of the curriculum as with the volume and pace of work and the cognitive saturation generated by sustained effort. Pupil disengagement in its variety of forms can therefore be understood as a pupil strategy which they appear to use, in a surprisingly conscious way, to liberate themselves from the boredom which characterises part, if not much, of their school day.

Apart from boredom, three pupils explained their disengagement specifically with reference to pupil/teacher relationships, though a number of pupils in the cohort made comments about this issue and expressed various concerns about teachers in general.

Hannah, for instance, spoke repeatedly of her 'hatred' for her class teacher Mrs Mitchell. She generally referred to her as 'Bossy Boots' and described how the teacher would 'shout' at her and tell her to 'sit down' when she sought help with her work. She also commented upon Mrs Mitchell's constant physical presence at her table monitoring her behaviour, and described how pleased she felt when the teacher moved away, so she could 'have more fun'.

Andrew's personal relationship with his teacher was far more positive than Hannah's, but he expressed reservations about teacher behaviour in general and suggested that it can have a direct impact on pupil behaviour. According to his analysis, teachers are often busy marking or dealing with problems, and so unavailable to help pupils when they are stuck. This means that pupils cannot progress with their work and are at a loose end. This, he argues, sets the stage for disengagement. Andrew put it as follows: 'Sometimes pupils are just mucking about, right, just making fun, and at times, right, the teacher says: 'Just get on with your work!' and, like, you're trying to explain... saying you were stuck, and the teacher didn't help you because it's a long queue'. Andrew also complained that teachers do not always 'listen to you', 'understand you', or 'believe your point of view'. He appeared to be suggesting that, in a climate like this, it is difficult for pupils to have their say and justify their behaviour to teachers. Michael and Ian expressed similar perceptions.

Four of the pupils in the cohort specifically categorised teachers as either 'shouters' or 'non-shouters', shouters being perceived as the teachers who raise their voices to admonish pupils for their behaviour. Shouters, from pupil points of view, tend to be unjust and punitive and were the unpopular teachers in this cohort. The pupils who identified their teachers as shouters all considered themselves as having very poor relationships with them. By contrast, three pupils specifically categorised their teachers as 'good' and 'nice', linking these labels to qualities of friendliness, fairness, understanding, and jokeyness. They observed that nice teachers will 'tick you off' or 'give you a row', but the way this is done is qualitatively different to the shouter approach and pupils could accept it. Thus, a pupil's sense that the teacher is going to be fair and basically supportive of them appeared to be crucial to pupil perceptions of teacher response and to the quality of the relationship that developed between them.

Michael, for example, was frightened by his teacher's shouting. He said: 'Sometimes when the class teacher shouts at me it makes me feel like I'm going to have a heart attack. I get a big fright'. He also complained that she sends him to 'stand under the clock' when he doesn't finish his work. Ian complained repeatedly that his teacher 'shouts', 'nags' and 'tells lies' about him, and his dislike of her was almost palpable. For example, he called her a 'pig' in his conversations with me, and when her back was turned he would sometimes pretend to shoot her with his fingers shaped into the barrel of a gun. His teacher never realised what was going on.

Andrew, Frank and David, on the other hand, adored their teacher, Mrs Parker. They were unanimous in the view that she was 'good' and 'nice', and they respected her for her kindness and understanding. For example, David noticed that she never told him off when he chatted but would quietly come over and sit near his table. She also gave him 'more time to do the work' and regularly said 'Well done David!' at the end of the day. Frank said: 'I like my teacher a lot. She's always nice to you, but if you do something bad she will tick you off. She makes jokes sometimes and is friendly. She gives you nice homework.'

These findings suggest that teacher style is highly salient to certain pupils. Most of the pupils in the Sommerville study preferred a teacher they perceived as supportive, positive and fair-minded to one who shouted and responded in ways they perceived as unfair. However, three of the pupils in the cohort expressed no opinion whatever on this matter. So it is not possible to generalise the findings across the cohort, nor clarify why teacher response is salient in some cases and not in others.

A few pupils in the group explained their disengagement with reference to relationships with peers. They squarely blamed their classmates for rejecting them and causing their disengagement by talking to them or getting them into trouble in various ways i.e. they perceived this influence as a context factor. By contrast, other pupils recognised that their active involvement with peers was the real cause of the problem, and blamed themselves rather than blaming others i.e they perceived it as a self factor. Indeed those in the latter category, like Gary, Andrew and Edward, all agreed that habit partly explained their behaviour. They described these habits as compulsive and difficult to resist.

Gary, for instance, said that he found talking completely irresistible! He confessed: 'I just can't shut my mouth!' Edward also declared that he was unable to 'resist the temptation' of chatting and socialising with friends though he acknowledged that it prevented him from getting on with his work. He said: 'I try to (work), but then, it's like, I hang around the people that are bad and then I get into trouble and just start being stupid again'. Andrew's habitual form of disengagement was referred to as 'chucking'. This entailed flicking maths cubes at the ceiling on the end of a ruler! Andrew claimed to find this activity thrilling and difficult to resist in moments of boredom. He spoke at great length about it, and with great animation and enthusiasm for his subject! He was delighted by the fun and laughs that chucking generated, both for him and for the rest of the class.

Another pertinent self factor – for Frank, John, Michael and Gary – was fatigue. Michael explained that he felt tired in the classroom because he often 'can't get to sleep 'till twelve o'clock because ...my brother keeps talking and the telly is on'. Frank had similar problems. Gary mentioned that he found it much easier to get on with his work and be a 'good' pupil 'when I'm not tired'. John admitted that he 'stays up a bit late' and is 'always tired'. This tiredness exacerbated John's tendency to abandon learning when he got 'fed-up'.

These quotes demonstrate that from pupil points of view pupil disengagement is not simply a defiant or gratuitous avoidance of learning. Rather, specific context factors, such as boredom, problems with the curriculum and pupil/teacher relationships are attributed by pupils as the causes or origins of their disengaged behaviour. Self factors, such as compelling, habitual behaviours and fatigue are also cited as significant, and seem to work in conjunction with context factors to amplify disengagement. Thus pupil explanations are generally overdetermined i.e. they refer to multiple influences, rather than to a single cause or origin, to explain their disengagement.

Disengagement for this particular group of pupils might therefore be understood as being driven by two underlying and complimentary purposes:

> **Purpose 1** – to achieve relief from uncomfortable learning experiences and feelings
>
> **Purpose 2** – to find a reliable means of having fun and time out

Viewed in this way, pupil disengagement, in this study at least, was always subjectively purposeful. We explore these purposes further in the next chapter.

Teacher explanations

Overall, teacher explanations for pupil disengagement had little in common with pupil or parent explanations. Table 2 on page 36 indicates that the range

Table 2: Teacher explanations

Number of teachers	No of pupil cases	Explanations
		Self Factors
5	8	Deficit explanations (attitude, ability, personality, etc.)
3	4	Family background
		Contract Factors
1	2	Peer factors
1	1	School changes
1	1	Relation with teacher
1	1	Teacher mismanagement

of teacher explanations (six) was far narrower than the range of pupil explanations (twelve). This is, perhaps, a surprising finding since one might expect teachers to have a greater capacity than pupils for generating explanations.

When the teacher explanations were categorised into context factors and self factors, it became clear that the teachers, unlike the pupils, were far more likely to attribute pupil disengagement to self factors. These self factors included personal deficits (in attitude, personality or ability), and, to a lesser extent, problems in family background. All five teachers in the cohort explained the behaviour of at least one of their pupils in terms of personal deficits i.e. behaviours that the teachers appeared to perceive as an intrinsic aspect of pupil character or personality, with the implication that it was either innate or had been learnt and become fixed at a very young age. Two examples illustrate this.

Mrs Johnson, for instance, identified a 'trait' in Gary she had 'seen before in certain boys and girls' and which she appeared to consider innate or at least intrinsic. Mrs Johnson explained that pupils with this trait: '...don't seem to see the need to conform like others, they don't seem to see that rules apply to them'. She continued: 'I've had [Gary] for almost half the year. For the first few months we were sussing each other out, seeing, to a certain extent, how far the rule can bend. Possibly by the time he's ready to move on to another teacher, we'll have worked out ground rules that suit us both.' This seems to suggest that the trait Mrs Johnson perceived in Gary was extremely robust, making him far more resistant to the processes that, for most pupils, lead to conformity to classroom rules.

Mrs Parker explained Andrew's disengagement in terms of a deficit of memory. Though she stressed that Andrew's 'memory problem' was not 'anything medical', there was a definite sense in which it was perceived as a robust and fixed feature of Andrew's functioning. Mrs Parker suggested that dealing with his poor memory would have to be a 'way of life' for Andrew and that he will always have to rely on strategies for working and remembering things, and will have to carry some sort of notebook to support his poor memory.

Family background was another key explanation used by teachers. For example, Mrs Watson partially attributed both Edward's and John's disengagement to their family background. She made sense of Edward's behaviour very much in terms of the reputation of his family, especially that of his older brother who had a turbulent career at Sommerville. Mrs Watson felt that Edward's poor attitude towards authority and his persistent disengagement had been learnt within his family. She suggested that their negative influence would be difficult for Edward to overcome. She said: 'There's a family history there ... I think [Edward's] probably fighting a losing battle.'

Mrs Watson also explained John's disengagement with reference to family background. For instance, she referred to 'problems at home' that might be influencing his responses in the classroom, and also speculated about the quality of parental care. She said: 'I just wonder how well stimulated John's been at home as a child, and whether he's been shown what's appropriate behaviour and what is not.' She also wondered whether John and his sister were 'shoved out of the way' to play on their own. Though Mrs Watson confessed that she 'doesn't know' how accurate her speculations are, she seemed quite assured in her belief that family background would be having some effect. She stated: '...a lot of what happens at home must affect the children. It's bound to, you know'. Two other teachers in the cohort agreed with her and provided similar explanations for pupil disengagement.

Overall, then, teacher explanations were dominated by self factors such as pupil deficits and family background and tended to be less overdetermined than pupil explanations. Teachers placed the causes or origins of pupil disengagement within the realms of innate personality or the psychological sphere, with the implication that they were beyond the direct influence of classroom and teacher. Many of these explanations seemed to go well beyond the immediate evidence of the classroom and were not consciously and deliberately checked out with those who might be able to confirm or negate their validity. They were rather like working hypotheses, based on teacher personal theories, which seemed coherent and plausible and enabled the teachers to get on and deal with the array of confusing behaviours in front of them. However, they were acted upon as if they were self-evidently true and their pupils had to live with the consequences.

Unlike pupils, teachers did not explain pupil behaviour with reference to the curriculum at all. There appeared to be a polarisation of pupil and teacher explanations that is typical of what is referred to in psychology as a classic 'attributional bias'. The attributional bias describes a statistically common pattern of explanation whereby individuals show a tendency to attribute their own behaviour to factors outside themselves – just as pupils explained their behaviour mainly in terms of learning context – whilst others attribute it to factors within the individual – just as teachers explain pupil behaviour in terms of pupil self.

Teachers did not appear to be aware that teacher response, especially shouting, could be problematic from pupil points of view. None of the teachers categorised themselves specifically as shouters, though two teachers categorised themselves as having a confrontational style of teaching characterised by a focus on 'firm discipline' and 'conformity' in the classroom. Since, with the exception of Mrs Parker, the teachers in the cohort did not consult their pupils about their disengagement, they were wholly unaware of their pupil's categorisations of teacher behaviour. Consequently, they could not use this information to supplement, or challenge, their own explanatory frameworks.

Parent explanations

The data in Table 3 opposite shows that parents, like pupils, expressed a wide range of explanations for pupil disengagement – fifteen in total. This range included many factors that were not mentioned by pupils or teachers, for example, writing posture, school standards, undiagnosed learning difficulties and transition problems.

However, a comparison of pupil, teacher and parent explanations suggests that there was some limited parent/pupil commonality, with a shared focus on context factors such relationship with teachers and peers. This may reflect the underlying influence of the pupil/parent relationship and the possibility of the mediation of perceptions. One parent, Mrs Dobson, stated this directly and said she knew that her son, Michael, was bored with his schoolwork because he regularly complained about it to her. She said: '...at the moment, [Michael's] version is that school's boring. That's how he sees it. No matter what we tell him, he says it's boring'.

Table 3: Parent explanations

Number of parents	Explanations
5	Peer group factors (context factor)
4	Pupil/teacher relationship (context factor)
3	Family background (self factor)
3	Deficit explanations (attitude, personality, etc) (self factor)
2	Boredom with curriculum (context factor)
1	Cognitive saturation (context factor)
1	Writing posture (self factor)
1	Teaching methods (context factor)
1	Pace of work (context factor)
1	School changes (context factor)
1	School standards (context factor)
1	Speech difficulty (early years) (self factor)
1	Transition to junior level (context factor)
1	Undiagnosed specific learning difficulty (self factor)
1	Teacher behaviour management (context factor)

But, it is also striking that some of the categories of explanation that recurred amongst parents were similar to those most numerous amongst teachers i.e. family background and pupil deficits. However, the emphasis was completely different. Parents' explanations overall were far less polarised than pupils' and teachers'. Thus, whereas teachers clearly tended to favour self factors, and pupils tended to favour context factors, parent explanations showed a mixture of both. The following examples illustrate the diversity of parent explanations.

Mrs Young, Mrs Lane, Mrs Anderson and Mrs Dobson all explained their children's disengaged behaviour with reference to the poor pupil/teacher relationship, and implicated teacher behaviour as a highly significant contributory factor.

For example, Mrs Dobson believed that her son Michael had a problematic relationship with his teacher Mrs Reid. She proposed that Mrs Reid was a 'shouter' and suggested that this 'frightened' her son as well as other pupils in the class and discouraged Michael from seeking assistance with work. When she tried to raise this issue directly with the teacher her perceptions were dismissed. This left Mrs Dobson in a state of uncertainty. She explained: 'There's been times I've said: "Well, did you ask the teacher?" and [Michael] says you get into trouble if you do this or if you speak out, you get into trouble. But then, [the teacher] says that's not true, so I don't know.' She went on: 'I don't think Michael is all wrong – maybe she's not all wrong either. But I do think she shouts, and I do think she's quite sharp with them.' Mrs Dobson felt that it was unfortunate that since his early years in primary school her son had had so many teachers who were 'more abrupt, more stern'. She believed this might have alienated him from learning from a young age.

Mrs Anderson echoed many of the comments recorded above. She has always found that her son Frank's behaviour and academic progress in the classroom were closely linked to how his teachers responded to him. She felt that he had, on the whole, been 'incredibly lucky' to have had 'really good teachers who really liked him'. But he did have one teacher who would 'shout at him and shame him' and she noted that Frank 'wasn't terribly happy' in her class, and made no academic progress at all. She concluded: '...if [Frank] got [a teacher] who wasn't sympathetic to him he wouldn't do very well. He doesn't have the resilience to deal with it.'

Mrs Lane also complained about the effect of teacher negativity on her son's classroom experiences. She felt that Ian's teachers never understood the effect of his speech and hearing problems when he entered primary one. Instead, they blamed Ian, and herself, for his poor behaviour and lack of progress in the classroom. On one occasion when she tried to defend Ian, a teacher told her: 'Well, he's a bad boy anyway, you can't get away from that'. Mrs Lane believed that this summed up teacher attitudes towards Ian and confirmed that they labelled him a 'bad boy' from early on in his school career. She believed that as a result Ian always identifies himself as 'the bad boy in the class'.

These quotations indicate how strongly certain parents felt about teacher behaviour towards their children. Their comments suggest that shouting, in particular, is negatively perceived by parents and is considered to be detrimental to pupil behaviour and performance. Two parents noted that teachers denied that they shout, directly contradicting the perceptions of their children. However, one parent associated his son's disengagement with a lack of authority in the classroom, and a general failure in the system as a whole to nip behaviour problems in the bud. This parent felt that a return to a more authoritarian regime in the classroom might be beneficial.

Parents also cited pupil relationship with their peers as a significant explanation for their child's disengagement. They sometimes linked this to character traits and pupil personality, but focused also on the potential of peers to be a constant distracting influence in the classroom. Indeed, they tended to see peers as the cause of disengagement, and their children as passive victims of the peer group dynamic. Mr and Mrs Findlay, Mrs Dobson, Mrs Young and Mrs Lane all referred to the peer group influence in this way.

Mrs and Mrs Findlay pointed out that John, for instance, 'likes to have an audience' and will do whatever his friends ask him to do. Thus '...if his friends are sitting making faces, he'll do it...If he's got an audience or someone telling him to do it, he'll do it.' They felt that John would always play up to his audience at the expense of learning. Mrs Dobson suggested that Michael was impressionable in this way too.

Mrs Young and Mrs Lane, however, felt that their children's learning in the classroom suffered for rather different reasons – because their peers had rejected them. Mrs Lane suggested that Ian was rejected way back in the first year of primary school when speech and hearing problems meant that he was difficult to communicate with and understand. She recalled that Ian was 'picked on' at the time, and she felt that 'people used to stay away from him because they couldn't have a normal conversation with him.' She proposed that her son's intense dislike of school started then, and she was aware that his relationship with his peers continued to be strained and conflictual.

Mrs Young suggested that Hannah had been regularly bullied at school, and though the teachers at Sommerville had tried to attend to the situation, Hannah reported that she continued to be 'picked on'. Mrs Young noted that Hannah's peers 'didn't play with her', and that she tended to gravitate towards younger children in the playground. Mrs Young concluded that Hannah's lack of friends in the classroom had undermined her enjoyment of school in general, and was another reason why she regularly 'called a sickie'.

Overall, parents, like pupils, tended towards multiple rather than singular explanations for their child's disengagement, attributing a number of causes from a far wider range than that proposed by teachers. This characteristic of parent explanations possibly reflects the far broader perspective they can bring to bear on an analysis of their child's behaviour, which includes insights mediated by both teachers and pupils. This may account for the blend of context and self factors favoured by parents. It also suggests, as we shall see, that they may have a valuable role to play in collaborative discussions of pupil behaviour in the classroom.

Conclusion

The results of the Sommerville study provide a powerful illustration of the multiple realities that exist within the primary classroom, and the inherent inadequacy of 'the view from nowhere' i.e. the view from a *teacher only* point of reference.

The findings indicate that the pupils in this study perceived their disengagement predominantly as a welcome relief from the boredom and frustration of the curriculum, and the uncomfortable feelings aroused by teachers and learning. In some respects they therefore evaluated their disengagement positively, though all the pupils acknowledged that it caused them to fall behind with their work and undermined their progress at school. They also acknowledged that it lead directly, in most cases, to conflict with teachers.

Teachers, by contrast, generally applied a deficit model to their perceptions of disengagement, and understood pupil behaviour largely as the result of problems in the pupils themselves or in their family backgrounds. They evaluated disengagement negatively. Further, all the teachers, with the exception of Mrs Parker, seemed to miss or dismiss the significance of pupil feeling states, and, somewhat surprisingly, overlooked the possibility that the curriculum they offered might be boring and demotivating for disengaging pupils. They did not appear to acknowledge that their own behaviour and responses in the classroom might also be part of the problem.

Parents, on the other hand, seemed to occupy a rather complex position in relation to disengagement. This is linked to their lack of direct experience of disengagement in the classroom and their reliance on perceptions mediated by teachers and their children. Parents were rather like the piggy in the middle. They seemed to see some aspects of the situation from their children's point of view – especially their feelings and the explanations for disengagement linked to teacher behaviour and the curriculum. But other aspects of their perceptions, such as those relating to descriptions of surface behaviour, tended to have more in common with teacher points of view.

The findings confirm how pupil, teacher and parent perceptions converge and collide in relation to disengagement, and illustrate the striking lack of intersubjectivity that can prevail. They provide firm support for the view that a more collaborative approach to behaviour problems in the classroom is worthy of consideration. However, this presents a considerable challenge to the way that behaviour is currently conceptualised in schools, and managed by teachers.

The next chapter teases out some of the issues raised by these findings via a more detailed examination of the predicament of the pupils in the study. We return to the predicament of the teachers and parents later on. Some elucidation is offered of the underlying purposes of pupil disengagement. This is set within the context of a broad review of the educational research within the field of pupil perceptions.

The idea of pupil survival strategies is introduced. A model of disengagement and intervention emerges from the discussion that might help teachers to clarify the phased and cyclical nature of the disengagement they regularly witness. This model is developed over the coming chapters, as teacher and parent dimensions are added, and our understanding of the intersubjective nature of disengagement deepens.

3

Watch my lips:
learning from pupil perceptions

What would happen if we treat the student as someone whose opinion mattered? (Fullan, 1991 p170)

Pupils spend a great deal of time in school. If, as we have seen, school life is problematic for disengaging pupils, filled with hours of boredom and confusion and with persistent rows and failures, it is not difficult to imagine how each day must cast a long shadow before them. It is almost surprising that more of these pupils do not follow Hannah's example and 'call a sickie'. It makes sense in the light of pupil perceptions. It is also one of few options open to pupils who have no real power to question and transform their circumstances in the primary classroom.

However, it says a lot that the vast majority of pupils do not take this option. Instead the Sommerville pupils, and many others like them, turn up at school day in and day out only to re-enact their idiosyncratic patterns of disengagement and endure the inevitable consequences. They are effectively trapped in an unhealthy and relentless downward spiral. Why do they persist? The answer, should we listen to pupils, is right in front of us. However it requires, as the quote above suggests, that we treat each pupil as someone whose opinion matters.

The Sommerville study discussed in chapter two was essentially an attempt to do just that – to take ten pupils seriously and to listen carefully to what they had to say. Their perceptions revealed that, whilst each pupil had their own unique experience of disengagement, they also had many opinions, beliefs and experiences in common. Social constructivist theory would suggest that this is because they were all children of a similar age who attended the same school. They were likely to have been exposed to similar beliefs about pupil role and behaviour in the classroom, especially those conveyed by their parents, teachers, peers, and the media. More significantly, all these pupils found themselves in a similar predicament as regards learning. As a result, an analysis of their perceptions revealed that their disengaged behaviour was underpinned by two complementary purposes:

> **Purpose 1**: to provide instant relief from difficult learning experiences and negative feeling states
>
> **Purpose 2**: to create enjoyable displacement activities (e.g. socialising, wandering around, playing, daydreaming) and positive feeling states

So disengagement, from the pupils' points of view, was a solution rather than a problem. Teachers, as we know, tend to see this the other way around. And this polarisation may help to explain the fundamental clash at the heart of the relationship between disengaging pupils and their teachers, with pupils seeking to preserve and perpetuate the very behaviours their teachers seek to control and eliminate.

Later in this chapter we explore a model of pupil and teacher interaction in the primary classroom that maps out this essentially contradictory relationship between pupil disengagement and teacher intervention. First, however, we consider pupil purposes and explore how they reflect the findings in the wider research on pupil perspectives. This will help us to grasp the deeper meaning of disengagement for primary pupils and appreciate how underlying meanings drive their behaviour forward, despite the negative consequences that invariably ensue. It may help answer the vexed question of why pupils like those in the Sommerville study are invariably so intransigent. Why are their patterns of disengagement so incredibly robust?

Purpose 1 – Relief from difficult learning experiences and negative feeling states

The curriculum

Pupil explanations for their disengagement tended to cluster more around context factors than self factors. There was a general consensus that problems with the curriculum lay at the heart of the matter, and boredom with lessons was repeatedly cited. It is notable that this boredom was associated principally with formal writing tasks rather than more active learning experiences. According to the literature, this is a common finding amongst pupils who are underachieving (Riley and Rustique-Forrester, 2002; Riley and Docking, 2004). Indeed, it is a common finding amongst pupils in general (Keys *et al*, 1995, Pollard and Triggs, 2000).

For example, Pollard and Triggs (2000) report on a large scale qualitative study of pupil perceptions of the curriculum that was conducted as part of the PACE project (Primary Assessment, Curriculum and Experience). Significant numbers of pupils in their study reported that they did not always find writing tasks enjoyable. This was associated with their perceptions of the volume of writing they had to deal with, and the amount of time and energy required to complete such tasks. Like the pupils in the Sommerville study, the PACE pupils highlighted their preference for active learning experiences over more formal learning tasks, and perceived active learning as a 'source of enjoyment' and 'a release from work' (*ibid*, p77).

The opposition, for pupils, between active learning as 'fun' *vis-à-vis* formal learning as 'work' has been uncovered by a number of researchers (Facer *et al*, 2003). For example, Wing (1995) and Sherman (1997) both conducted qualitative studies of pupil perceptions of the curriculum in nursery and infant classrooms and report similar findings. They comment upon the fact that on entry to school, young children are quickly socialised into the language of learning as 'work' as opposed to 'play'. Culturally speaking, the dominant notion of play, especially beyond the very early years of school, is that it is largely 'non-productive' and 'insignificant' and something that should be marginal to the serious enterprise of learning as 'work' (Sherman, 1997, p122). Pupils soon learn to apply these constructions and understand that the directed, obligatory and rather bland nature of much schoolwork is its main distinguishing feature (Wing, 1995).

Sherman goes on to comment upon the distinctive loss this represents to many young pupils and the 'drudgery', as pupils see it, of much classroom work (Sherman, 1997, p122). She notes that this loss is heightened, for some pupils, on transition into the junior years when play suddenly takes a dramatic step out of the classroom and learning as work shifts into a much higher gear. Her insights appear to reflect the sense of loss articulated by those pupils in the Sommerville study who expressed a palpable yearning for play. Sherman concludes that the integration of work and play throughout the school years would make learning more enjoyable for all. This solution, no doubt, would be much appreciated by the Sommerville pupils.

However it should be stressed that, despite their many problems with the more formal school curriculum, all the pupils in the Sommerville study could identify at least one subject they enjoyed. Significantly, PE and music were the most popular subjects, and drawing and active learning experiences the most popular classroom tasks. They tended to be associated with improved engagement. By contrast, writing, and to a lesser extent maths, were the least popular subjects and were associated with increased disengagement. Thus the pupils in the research cohort could not be said to be anti-learning *per se*. Rather, they seemed to have a strong preference for learning in particular ways in particular areas of the curriculum.

Again, these findings are fairly typical across the research literature. For example, Gardner (1993) explores the subject of the school curriculum in some depth and argues that the linguistic and logico-mathematical modes of learning that dominate western education directly disadvantage pupils whose talents and preferences lie in other modes. He initially categorised these modes as spatial, musical, bodily kinaesthetic, interpersonal and intra-personal, but later added the naturalistic mode. He proposes that these modes are all associated with specific 'intelligences' that are currently marginalised and undervalued in western schooling. It is interesting that the curriculum preferences within the pupil cohort fall exactly within these marginal zones.

Gardner's work is not without its detractors and there has been some serious and justifiable questioning of the exact meaning of his notion of multiple intelligences. Nonetheless, his work has attracted great interest. This is possibly linked to the fact that it resonates perfectly with what pupils tell us about their perceptions of the curriculum. It also reflects the experiences of many class teachers.

Thus there appears to be some agreement amongst primary pupils, and within the educational community in general, that there is a profound bias built into the primary school curriculum, with its emphasis on formal learning and its associations with work, that might account for the boredom and frustration experienced by many pupils. This implies, as the Sommerville pupils suggest, that the nature of the school curriculum itself could account, at least in part, for pupil disengagement.

However, the lack of fun was not their only criticism of the curriculum. One pupil in the cohort specifically explained his disengagement with reference to the level of difficulty of the work. Other pupils in the cohort stated that they found formal work 'difficult'. This term is an ambiguous one, as it may be used by pupils to mean that they feel they lack the ability to cope with a task – i.e. they can't do it. On the other hand, it can simply mean that are unwilling, rather than unable, to engage with a task – i.e. they lack the motivation to do it. Follow-up statements such as 'I can't be bothered' (Hannah) or '...it goes on too long...' (Michael, John, Ian) suggested that, for these pupils at least, a lack of motivation may have played the greater part. Their statements also suggest that their tendency to give up easily was inextricably linked to context factors such as length of task, problems generating ideas, cognitive saturation, volume and pace of work etc. Some pupils referred directly to these factors when explaining their disengagement.

Participant observation supported their comments. For example, when questioned about the task in hand during lessons, the Sommerville pupils generally understood what they had been asked to do and could explain it accurately to the researcher. They could also identify how they ought to be approaching the task. Thus, in the majority of cases, motivation, rather than ability, appeared to be the underlying barrier to engagement.

Up until recently, our understanding of pupil motivation has largely been constructed by adults via the study and dissemination of teacher and researcher assessments of pupil motivation. Though such constructions may provide valid and useful ways of making sense of pupil behaviour, an important argument throughout this book is that adult-centred perspectives constitute only a partial and selective view of the situation. Unfortunately, however, there are few pupil-centred studies of motivation in the literature to counterbalance this bias. Those that do exist tend to confirm a positive association between low motivation and pupil disengagement (e.g. Soloman and Rogers, 2001) and suggest that some pupils acknowledge that their own lack of effort can have a bearing on their learning. For the Sommerville pupils, this lack of effort appeared to be closely linked in their minds to the content and presentation of the curriculum.

Pollard and Tann's research suggested that mainstream pupils often share these concerns about the curriculum. If this is true, why is it that the vast majority of them accept the situation and do not go on to disengage? It seems clear that there must be some reason why the pupils in the Sommerville study took the crucial step of refusing formal learning and opting for disengagement. Their disaffection with the curriculum only provides part of the answer.

Relationships with teachers and peers

Some pupils in the Sommerville cohort blamed teachers or peers for their disengagement in the classroom. Those who blamed teachers were particularly aggrieved by those they categorised as 'shouters'. Pupils suggested that shouters provoked fear, anxiety, resentment and even hatred. Shouting therefore seemed to undermine pupil well being, compromised cooperation, and contributed to the development of a generally negative and reactive orientation towards school. Teachers who did not shout, by contrast, were distinctly popular. Mrs Parker springs to mind here. Indeed, teachers who stood out as non-shouters appeared to have been an important source of comfort to certain pupils in the Sommerville study. Hannah and Ian, for example, spoke with enormous affection of teachers who were kind, gentle and caring towards them. They continued to visit these teachers at playtime and would chat to them in the corridor despite having moved on from their classrooms many years ago.

Once again, these findings largely fall in line with other studies in the field of pupil disaffection (McManus, 1995, Riley and Docking, 2004). In a broad review of the literature McManus (1995) suggests that there are certain characteristics of teacher behaviour and response that all pupils appear to appreciate. These include fairness and friendliness, informality and humour, and a respect and interest in pupils as individuals. Pupils also value teachers who maintain class control and provide interesting lessons (p112-113). McManus points out, however, that teachers who do not possess these qualities are likely to be unpopular. He suggests that it is not uncommon for disaffected pupils to blame such teachers for their problems in the classroom.

These findings are also reflected in the PACE study of pupil perceptions. Kindness and friendliness were highly valued by the older primary pupils. 'Making jokes, having a laugh and being fun' were also important qualities of popular teachers (*ibid*, p110), as were firm control and good order in the classroom. Like the Sommerville pupils, the PACE pupils agreed that they preferred teachers who did not shout and with whom they were able, to some degree, to negotiate in the classroom. Interestingly, however, the vast majority of PACE pupils indicated that they were happy, ultimately, to submit to teacher control. Indeed, they affirmed that they tried to avoid confrontations with teachers wherever possible. The authors comment:

> There is a strong sense here of children who have learned to live with 'the way it is', who have accepted a particular construction of the role of 'teacher'. There are also indications of a tacit negotiation between teachers and pupils. For the pupils, acceptance was conditional on factors such as 'fairness', teacher personality or a level of demand they found acceptable. However, among the reasons given for acceptance of teacher authority, the fear of exposure, when expressed, was ... strong.' (Pollard and Triggs, 2000 p123)

Here, then, is where the Pace pupils and the Sommerville pupils part company, for it is clear that whereas the majority of the pupils in the PACE project were likely to accept teacher power and feared the consequences of an overt challenge to teacher authority, pupils in the Sommerville study were characterised by their willingness to take the teacher on and over-ride teacher directives. These pupils were clearly not deterred by fear of exposure. This may well account for the highly robust nature of pupil disengagement.

A few of the pupils in the Sommerville cohort also talked about difficulties in their relationship with peers in the classroom. Some linked these difficulties directly to their disengaged behaviour. They focused specifically on the negative influence of peers on their learning and sometimes blamed peers for 'deliberately' getting them into trouble and distracting them from work. There were also concerns about peer rejection, conflictual relationships with classmates and problems collaborating with others during group learning tasks. These pupils perceived their peers as one of the many causes of their problems in the classroom.

According to the research, a pupil's relationship with their peers is often a litmus test of their social and psychological adjustment and is widely considered to be a significant factor in the development of problems in the classroom (Laird *et al*, 2001). Indeed, the links between peer relations, peer rejection and behaviour are well established in the literature (Cooper, 2006). Pollard and Triggs (2000) make the important point that peer relationships are significant for most pupils in the primary classroom, not just disengagers, and are an important signifier of social status amongst pupils. They suggest that those who are isolated from their peers are likely to be outsiders with low social status and poor self-esteem, and are at particular 'risk of a negative spiral' that undermines pupil identity and compounds difficulties with learning (p304).

Self factors
The pupils in the Sommerville study cited a number of highly idiosyncratic self factors to explain their disengagement in the classroom, such as the irresistible compulsion to talk, socialise or daydream. Interestingly, the pupils spoke of these behaviours as if they were beyond their control and impossible to regulate.

Soloman and Rogers (2001) conducted a study of secondary pupil's perceptions of their behaviour, and explored the factors that culminated in their placement in a special unit. These pupils also spoke of a set of 'uncontrollable aspects of themselves' that they felt contributed to their disengagement, though the behaviours they cited were completely different (*ibid,* p341). The authors conclude that their perceptions revealed a poor 'sense of agency' i.e. a lack of belief in the idea that they could do something to change their habits (*ibid,* p341). It might be argued that this underlying belief will have a significant bearing on the durability of pupil behaviour and might contribute to the robustness characteristic of disengagement.

The influence of fatigue upon learning was mentioned by a few pupils in the Sommerville cohort. Laziness and 'forgetting to be good' were also cited as explanations for disengagement. Though these self factors are highly idiosyncratic and are unlikely to have been researched, it is not difficult to accept that they might be significant to individual pupils and will undermine their performance and achievement in the classroom. Pupil insights such as this are of enormous value to teachers and supply them with important pieces of the jigsaw of disengagement. Their specificity enables teachers to begin to make sense of the unique inner world of the pupil that lies under the surface of classroom behaviour.

Pupil feeling states

The Sommerville pupils indicated that their responses in the classroom were accompanied by an array of negative feeling states specific to each individual. Feelings such as boredom, fear, resentment and hatred were all associated with the context and self factors explored above. The apparent salience of feeling states for the pupils in this study reflects, in part, the fact that they form a distinctive group of pupils in primary schools – pupils who, because of their persistent disengagement, regularly find themselves in direct conflict with teachers, peers, parents, and perhaps with themselves in relation to internalised expectations and aspirations. Emotional fallout linked to biographical factors such as problems at home were not directly addressed by this study but may have been significant in the underlying genesis of pupil emotions. Nonetheless, the discussion so far has rallied considerable evidence to suggest that there is a great deal about the context of the classroom itself that can trigger emotional reactions in pupils.

What seems to be distinctive about the Sommerville pupils is the vividness of their emotional experiences and their inability, or unwillingness, to cast negative emotions aside in order to focus upon academic tasks. The emotional content of pupil perceptions is, in many cases, expressed in powerful statements that appear to reflect the sheer force and immediacy of their emotional experiences. Ian and Hannah's comments about their hatred for their teachers are memorable examples. Riley and Docking (2004) also comment upon the 'powerful imagery' (p168) disaffected pupils use to express their feelings about school. They conclude that, for many pupils, this is because their experiences are 'profoundly sad and depressing' (p168).

The significance of emotional states for the Sommerville pupils stood out in sharp relief against the distinct lack of salience they had for most of the teachers in the study. However, the literature suggests that this finding reflects a general ambivalence towards childhood emotionality within school culture as a whole (Goleman, 1996). Baxter's (1999) study of the mental health assessments of four teachers in a London primary school appears to confirm this. She found that the teachers tended to under-report emotional symptoms amongst their pupils compared to other categories of pupil difficulty such as peer group problems, conduct problems and hyperactivity. Baxter makes the important point that the teachers did not seem to find it easy to identify and distinguish emotional behaviours.

Despite decades of research into child-centred education with its focus on the emotional needs of the child, this cultural deficit of emotional understanding now appears to be deeply entrenched in our education system. Trowell and Bower (1995) claim that the introduction of the 1988 Education Reform Act radically changed the climate of education in Britain. They suggest that the introduction of a market system of schooling has forced educators to emphasise quantitative measures of learning and behaviour and neglect more qualitative concerns. Budget restrictions have also ensured that support services are becoming increasingly fragmented and inefficient (*ibid*) with the effect that there is far less support and advice available to teachers and pupils struggling with emotional issues in the classroom.

However, this trend of emotional neglect is beginning to be questioned by researchers and educators working within the emergent field of emotional intelligence (Goleman, 1996). This term refers to the development of the human capacity to identify and control inner feelings and impulses, and the ability to identify, empathise with, and handle the feelings of others in ways that are constructive and healthy. Goleman quotes a great deal of American research that suggests that academic success is closely linked to emotional health from the earliest days of schooling. He asserts that 'intellect cannot work at its best without emotional intelligence' (Goleman, 1996, p28). If this is the case, pupil accounts of their negative emotional experiences might well provide a crucial key to their underachievement. Yet it is a key that most of the teachers in the Sommerville study did not grasp. There are many reasons why this is so, as we see in the next chapter. One important reason relates directly to the prevailing culture of schooling.

Donaldson (1992) suggests that, on entering school, most young pupils are socialised to put their emotional experience in brackets. They are taught, albeit implicitly, to ignore irrelevant distractions in the classroom in order to focus solely upon intellectual learning. This capacity, which she calls 'emotional disembedding', is intrinsic to success as a learner in our culture. This may explain why teachers often resent having to deal with emotional problems in the classroom and clarifies why they do not perceive this to be an integral feature of their professional role.

Donaldson's comments echo the findings of Jackson (1987), who conducted a small-scale interpretive study of the perceptions of pupils in two reception classes. This study is a much quoted early classic in pupil voice research, and continues to have much to tell us about the enculturation of pupils into mainstream schooling. Jackson found that pupils 'make sense' of school by slowly learning, adapting to, and integrating the implicit rules governing classroom life, especially the rules around 'how to be taught'. This rule is linked to the expectation that children will put current preoccupations aside in order to concentrate on learning. She emphasises:

> An important part of 'making sense of school' is learning to confine active learning to the constraints of the situation. (*ibid,* p85)

However, both Jackson and Donaldson warn that such adaptations are extremely difficult for some individuals, especially those whose past experiences and perspectives do not fit the predominantly middle class culture of the classroom. Donaldson points out that this difficulty may be greatest for children whose emotional lives are in distress, and for those who lack a strong, intrinsic sense of 'personal security' (Donaldson, 1992, p254). She suggests that such pupils may find it taxing to have to prise themselves away from emotional concerns and achieve the level of emotional control that teachers expect.

To add to this, though the requirement for emotional control is implied by the rule system of the classroom and is encouraged by most teachers, the skills and attitudes associated with emotional intelligence are not explicitly and systematically taught within primary education. The predicament of pupils with emotional concerns can therefore be exacerbated by the fact that teachers fail to comprehend the nature of their difficulties and do not provide appropriate support. To make matters worse, they may perceive a pupil's inability to make emotional adjustments as a problem located solely in the child. Teachers may not consider the possibility that it might also be inextricably linked to a serious gap in school provision. As we shall see, this misconception is common amongst several of the teachers in the Sommerville study.

It might therefore be argued that children could be more successful in meeting behavioural and performance expectations if teachers were more sensitive to pupil feelings and more skilful at teaching the subtle but complex art of disembedded learning. Jackson suggests that such sensitivity would 'help teachers to help children to become more effective classroom participants' (Jackson, 1987, p86). Research already indicates that teaching emotional literacy can lead to improvements in pupil behaviour (Wells *et al*, 2003; Weare and Gray, 2003).

Unfortunately, most of the Sommerville pupils lacked direct emotional support from their teachers – hence their dogged determination to seek relief from disagreeable feeling states via any means at their disposal. Disengagement was clearly an effective way of achieving this because it immediately and reliably insulated them, albeit only in the short term, from both problematic learning conditions and high levels of emotional dissonance. Disengagement therefore brought the relief that their teachers did not, or could not, provide.

Several pupils, backed up by their parents, explained that they began to experience emotional difficulties on entry to school. They reported feeling bewildered by the more formal aspects of schooling, feeling excluded by peers, and feeling frightened by teachers who shouted at them and did not seem to understand their problems. Hannah, Simon, Michael, Ian, David and Frank were all marked by early emotional upsets such as these. Their negative feelings were never directly addressed or resolved by their teachers but appear to have been compounded as they progressed up the school. It is likely, therefore, that the seeds of their disengagement were sown in the earliest years of their primary education.

Purpose 2: Creating opportunities for enjoyable displacement activities and positive feeling states

The Sommerville pupils painted a clear and detailed picture of the underlying problems that triggered their disengagement, launching them into patterns of behaviour involving persistent socialising, play, daydreaming, wandering around and other pleasurable forms of time wasting. Significantly, the research literature indicates that the active pursuit of these forms of fun and time out from learning are not peculiar to pupils who disengage in the classroom. On the contrary, there is wide acceptance of the fact that most primary and secondary pupils actually attend to two agendas as they go about the school day. One might be construed as the official agenda represented by, and transmitted through, teachers. The other is a more personal, pupil agenda that operates alongside the official one.

Researchers therefore agree upon the primacy of fun for many pupils, and the high priority given to having a laugh in the classroom. The vast majority of pupils explore this priority within distinct parameters that are implicitly shared and understood by pupils and teachers. They know that, within these parameters, certain forms of fun have a tacit legitimacy (Pollard, 1985). However, they also know that fun that pushes these limits is an entirely different matter. This subject is explored in the educational literature under the heading of 'pupil agendas' and is associated with accepted forms of 'coping' in the primary classroom (*ibid*).

Pupil agendas and coping in the classroom

Davies (1980) and Pollard (1985) both conducted seminal studies on the social life of the primary classroom that were based on pupil rather than adult perceptions of behaviour. Davies (1980) studied the perceptions of a group of nine and ten year old pupils in an Australian primary school setting. She focused upon their personal accounts of classroom interaction and claims that the social world of childhood is not abandoned at the classroom door. She suggests that most pupils become adept at negotiating the rules of adult and childhood culture simultaneously in the classroom and that pupils are generally proficient at 'switching' seamlessly between the two (Davies, 1980, p258). This facility enables pupils to participate in the teacher agenda necessary for their educational progress whilst seeing to childhood business such as socialising, squabbling, joking about. Most pupils appear able to do this without any disruption to their education and without any significant threat to pupil/teacher relationships. Davies observed:

> [The children] recognised that the successful carrying out of the teacher's agenda ... involved following the teacher's rules. Alongside the teacher's agenda, they quite busily pursued their own agenda, which related to matters specific to the culture of childhood ... Mucking around, and having fun and interacting with each other were as much, if not more, part of the school day as learning lessons ... For the children, freedom to pursue their own agendas was essential for the continued maintenance and construction of their shared worlds. (Davies, 1980, p265)

Pollard (1985) also studied pupil perceptions of the social world of the class-room, though his work took place in several primary schools in England. Like Davies, Pollard acknowledges that most pupils manage to negotiate the inter-actional rules of the classroom setting to ensure that their personal agendas are accommodated to some extent. He also emphasises the importance to children of learning, on the one hand, and peer group membership on the other. However, he suggests that the key to understanding pupil agendas lies in recognising their underlying function. He specifies this function as the 'protection of self' and suggests that pupils try to achieve this by prioritising enjoyment, controlling stress, maintaining their self-image and protecting their dignity. He refers to these four items as pupil 'interests-at-hand' i.e. their 'most significant and immediate concerns' in the primary classroom (*ibid*, p81).

Pollard recognises, however, that pupils in primary classrooms are not a homogeneous set. They approach the protection of self in a variety of dif-ferent ways. He identifies three pupil sub-cultures whose members employ distinct strategies for securing their interests-at-hand. 'Goodies', as he cate-gorises them, secure their interests by giving more priority to learning than to peer group membership. 'Gangs' give more priority to peer group member-ship than to learning, whilst 'Jokers' typically try to strike some sort of balance between the two. Pollard refers to these prototypical approaches as pupil 'coping strategies'. He defines this term as follows:

> A coping strategy ... is a type of patterned and active adaptation to a situation by which an individual copes. It is a creative but semi-routinised and situational means of protecting the individual's self. (Pollard, 1985, p155)

Pollard maintains that finding ways of making space for pupil agendas in the classroom is therefore not a trivial feature of pupil behaviour, but a vital aspect of coping at school for all pupils.

The Sommerville pupils: coping or surviving?

These findings have clear links with the outcomes of the Sommerville study in the sense that they confirm the ubiquity of the pupil agenda in the class-room. The interest-at-hand Pollard refers to as 'enjoyment' obviously mirrors the pupil purpose relating to the pursuit of fun and time out from learning. Further, the interest-at-hand he refers to as 'control of stress' could be linked to the pupil 'need for relief' from a variety of problematic context and self factors. It is also conceivable that both of the pupil purposes identified by this study are linked in some ways to what Pollard labels the 'maintenance of self-image' and 'retention of dignity', though it is not possible to relate this conclusively to the findings. Certainly, as Pollard claims, it is likely that both these purposes are of profound importance to protecting 'self' in some way.

However, there are some important differences between these pieces of research and the Sommerville study. For example, whilst Davies and Pollard regard both learning and peer group membership are vital organising principles in the lives of most pupils in the primary classroom, this did not appear to be the case for the Sommerville pupils. The opposite was more accurately the case since for these pupils the learning process had effectively broken down. Further, peer group membership was highly problematic for several pupils in the research group and, for the rest, it did not emerge as a major explanatory factor for their disengagement. Most of these pupils were rather marginal figures in the classroom. They tended to act alone rather than operating as if in one of Pollard's gangs.

As a corollary, Pollard's concept of coping does not appear to be wholly relevant to the ten pupils in the Sommerville study. They do not appear to fit into any of Pollard's sub-groups, nor do their behaviours resonate with the coping strategies associated with them. What stands out, rather, is the huge difference in priority that the pupils in this study gave to their own personal agendas in comparison to the rest of the pupils in their classrooms, and the pupils studies by Davies and Pollard. The sheer frequency and intensity of usage of their personal agendas is what characterised their disengagement and caused such problems for their teachers. This imbalance in priorities meant that the Sommerville pupils could not achieve the sort of harmonising of teacher and pupil agendas that Pollard claims most pupils seek. Hence the deterioration of the pupil/teacher relationship. Their personal agendas were also prioritised at the expense of their learning to such an extent that all ten pupils fell into a pattern of chronic underachievement that was difficult for them to escape. Any notion of coping therefore seems entirely aberrant in their case.

Instead, I would suggest that the adaptive strategy applied by the pupils in this study might more accurately be construed as a 'survival strategy'. This term has been used in numerous sociological studies of classroom interaction (e.g. Wood, 1977), but my use of the term here is somewhat different. Like a coping strategy, the survival mechanism I am speaking of seems to be 'patterned', 'semi-routinised' and 'situational' in accordance with Pollard's definition. In other words, the form of disengagement specific to each pupil tends to be repetitive, habitual and also closely associated with conditions within particular classroom environments. This accounts for the fact that pupil disengagement can change form, or even disappear, when the pupil is moved to a different context. However, the term 'survival' seems more apposite in the case of the Sommerville pupils because it conveys the idea of their desperate struggle to maintain their well-being and endure the school day, in the face of a chronic breakdown in their ability to cope like other pupils. What is really happening, and what their behaviour signifies, is that these particular pupils are not coping at all.

In almost every case, according to pupil reports, these survival strategies had taken a number of years to develop. In some cases they took seed on the very first day of school but were left unaddressed and evolved over time. Yet, pupils continued to pursue their idiosyncratic survival strategies at considerable cost to themselves. These costs were as follows:

- **learning suffered** – All the pupils in the cohort were fully aware that their disengagement caused them to experience difficulties in finishing their work and to fall behind their peers. They understood that this simply added to their learning problems and compounded their underachievement.

- **conflict** – All pupils confirmed that their disengagement provoked a response from the teacher. This response was usually confrontational (except in Mrs Parker's case). Disengagement also brought some, but not all, pupils into conflict with their parents and with their own internalised expectations and standards. In a few cases, conflict with peers also resulted.

- **relief was temporary** – Because teachers quickly intervened to put a stop to disengagement, pupils were repeatedly returned to work only to be confronted by their problems all over again. Thus, paradoxically, disengagement did not solve their problems for long. In fact it generally made matters worse in the long run.

As a result of these costs, half the pupils in the Sommerville cohort experienced at least some ambivalence about their disengaged behaviours. These pupils tended to articulate a teacher referenced value system characterised by teacher expectations and evaluations of their behaviour. They were concerned about the effect of disengagement on future academic outcomes. They were also interested in the possibility of change, though they were uncertain how it might be achieved.

By contrast, the other half of the pupils in the research cohort appeared not to experience such ambivalence. Though these pupils also expressed negative, teacher-referenced evaluations of their disengagement, and were clearly able to anticipate how they would be judged by other adults, para-doxically they also expressed very positive judgments of their disengagement and seemed to thoroughly enjoy it despite its temporary nature. They were unconcerned about the costs indicated above. Thus their views were pre-dominately pupil-referenced. These pupils tended to blame teachers and the curriculum for their problems, and felt that the onus was not on themselves to change, but on the school.

***

To summarise, then, from pupil points of view, disengagement might be con-strued as a survival strategy, characterised by repeated and sustained pupil disengagement at the point of learning. This pupil response represents an attempt to resolve two underlying and preoccupying pupil purposes: the desire for relief from underlying problems with learning and negative feel-ings, and a corresponding need for opportunities for enjoyment and time out.

This analysis suggests that the pupils in the Sommerville cohort disengaged because they had no other choice that would enable them to achieve these underlying purposes. Simply stopping the behaviour at the request of their teachers was not an option they could risk. The absence of any alternative that would meet their needs explains why they had to press on with their dis-engagement in the face of strong teacher opposition. As a corollary, lack of fear of teacher authority was integral, indeed, vital to the successful working of their survival mechanisms, for clearly fear, should they succumb to it, would have heralded the immediate collapse of their best, and only, means of relief. This process was confirmed by several pupils in the study. In chapter two, Michael, for example, provided a vivid description of his fear of his teacher, yet he never allowed this fear to deflect him from disengagement but became adept at quickly overriding it. For other pupils, such as Ian, any trace of fear, had it ever existed, had been subsumed by anger or in some cases an open and declared hostility towards their teachers. This hatred seems to have played an essential role in fuelling their ongoing opposition to learning.

Viewed in this way, chatting, playing, messing about and daydreaming argu-ably have a rational, and as Pollard suggests, self-protective function that may explain why pupils are so ardent in their pursuit of them. This, in turn, ex-plains why disengaged behaviours are invariably so difficult for pupils to re-linquish and for teachers to deal with. But we should remember that three pupils in the cohort significantly reduced their disengagement over the period of the research. All three were in Mrs Parker's class and, in terms of the logic set out above, were offered a viable alternative to disengagement. However, it is highly significant that this alternative was perceived by the pupils themselves as being supportive of, rather than threatening to, their underlying quest for survival in the classroom. In the following chapter we consider the elements of Mrs Parker's approach that enabled her pupils to safely release their hold on behaviours that, for several years, had undermined their achievement in school.

A model of disengagement and intervention

The discussion so far, based on pupil perspectives, casts considerable light on the inner workings of the clash between teachers and disengaging pupils in the primary classroom. And it highlights the poor quality of relationship that can emerge as a result. Structured observations of pupils and teachers in the classroom conducted during the Sommerville study suggested that this 'tug-of-war' between them (Goodnow and Burns, 1991) tended to occur in a surprisingly patterned way characterised by an evolution through four predictable phases:

Phase 1: Entry phase

This phase began when each pupil was introduced to a specific learning task and was characterised by the pupil's immediate response to teacher instructions. This usually took the form of an attempt to settle down, open the workbook, pick up a pencil and make a start on the task.

Phase 2: Disengagement

This phase began when the pupil started to show behaviours lasting more than a few minutes that were unrelated to the learning task. These behaviours were usually habitual and unique to the individual and entailed specific behavioural acts such as chatting, sharpening pencils, wandering around, playing, etc. Pupil feeling state tended to change in this phase, though this was not always discernable to others – e.g. feelings of boredom turned to enjoyment.

Phase 3: Intervention

This phase began when the teacher noticed pupil disengagement and intervened with the aim of bringing it to an end. The teacher's form of intervention was idiosyncratic and related to teacher style – e.g. shouter or non-shouter. Teacher feeling could sometimes be discerned in this phase – e.g. feelings of anger or frustration.

Phase 4: Response to intervention

This phase included the pupil acts and feeling states that arose directly after intervention. It generally included a period of reactivity (angry mumbling under the breath; a noisy and resentful return to task) followed by a more settled period and a quiet transition back into the cycle at phase 1. Depending on circumstances, the cycle would then begin again.

These four phases of disengagement and intervention were common to all of the pupils and teachers in the Sommerville study, though the details of their specific responses within each phase were unique to each dyad. This phased pattern might be represented as a cyclical model (see Figure 1 opposite).

This model is constructed as cyclical and dynamic rather than linear and static because an ongoing and repetitive movement through each phase was clearly observable in the Sommerville classrooms across the school day. Indeed, the ubiquity of these cycles, and the requirement to repeatedly deal with them, was what the teachers in the Sommerville study found so utterly exhausting. This feeling will surely resonate with any teacher who has experienced disengagement in the classroom.

In addition, structured observation suggested that each cycle seemed to continually reinforce and consolidate the disengagement of the pupil and the intervention of the teacher so that, over time, it evolved into an increasingly robust, predictable and habitual pattern. For some pupils in the Sommerville study, this pattern escalated over the research period as pupil and teacher responses intensified and became more oppositional. In other cases cycles weakened over time as pupils responded to positive intervention and feedback, and teacher/pupil behaviour patterns became more aligned and mutually beneficial.

In Figure 2 on page 64, this generalised model of disengagement and intervention has been applied to Sommerville pupil Michael Dobson and to his teacher Mrs Reid. Their perceptions have been used to flesh out the details within each phase of the cycle so that their specific pattern of disengagement and intervention can be represented. This representation, though simplified, enables us to conceptualise the interactive dynamic between pupil and teacher and begin the process of making sense of what is happening in the classroom.

At this stage the model merely maps the overt, observable interactive process. What is missing is any sense of how these surface patterns of behaviour are linked to underlying purposes. This link is crucially important because we

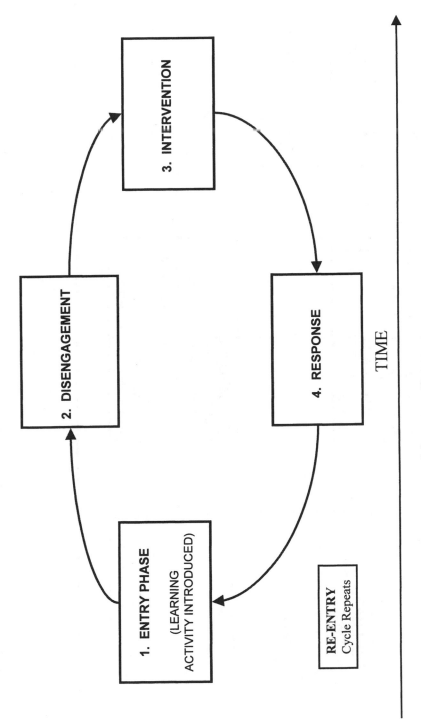

Figure 1: Cycle of disengagement and intervention

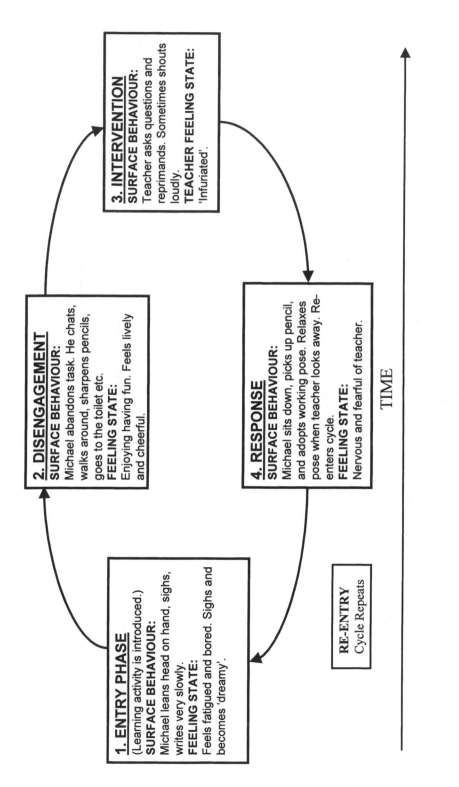

Figure 2: Michael's cycle of disengagement and intervention

know these purposes act rather like a dynamo that powers pupil cycles and drives them forward. So pupil purposes need to be integrated into the model.

Figure 3 on page 66 illustrates the dialectical relationship between Michael's underlying purposes and his surface behaviours. It also indicates how the costs of pupil disengagement feed back into pupil cycles and ensure that there is no halt or resolution to the ongoing dynamic. Though this model is applied to Michael for illustrative purposes, it could be applied to any of the pupils in the cohort, and by extension, to any pupil displaying disengaged behaviours. What matters is how each pupil's unique subjective perceptions fit into its phased structure.

This model has a practical function and might be used by teachers to clarify and map out the minutiae of pupil survival strategies. In order to make use of it, however, pupil perceptions would have to be taken seriously by teachers in the spirit that Fullan (1991) advocates at the start of this chapter. Further, and perhaps more importantly, it would require that teachers take the radical next step of acting, where appropriate, upon pupil points of view. It goes without saying that, without this step, the enterprise of collaborating with pupils becomes futile and meaningless.

Yet taking this step would represent a huge shift in practice for primary teachers who are currently locked into an adultist view of classroom behaviour. There are many personal, practical and pedagogical reasons why such teachers might resist this step and argue against it. The teachers in the Sommerville study highlighted a number of these arguments. The issue of the teacher's predicament as regards pupil disengagement is the main theme of the next chapter. This discussion will facilitate further elaboration of the model of disengagement and intervention to embrace teacher perspectives. It will also counter-balance the pupil focus emphasised so far by placing pupil perspectives within a broader context.

This principle of counter-balancing perspectives is important in collaborative practice and acts as an antidote to the tendency, within the educational research literature and beyond, to polarise the debate on pupil behaviour. This polarisation has resulted in the emergence of two discourses over recent years. One discourse takes a traditional teacher-centred focus and is concerned with the management and control of pupil behaviour by adults. The other locates itself within the literature on pupil voice and takes a pupil-centred stance. Both these perspectives are valuable to any discussion of pupil disengagement, thus a synthesis of these two positions needs to be considered. This makes sense within the framework of this book.

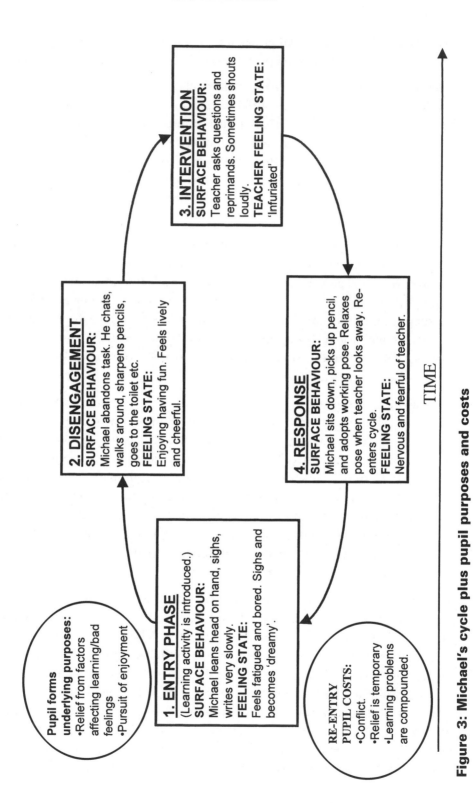

Figure 3: Michael's cycle plus pupil purposes and costs

So the next chapter acknowledges the impact of multiple perspectives within the collaborative classroom and begins to appreciate the complexities of classroom life that can get in the way of effective partnership.

4

Are they listening?
the teacher's predicament

> ...One must also listen to the voice of the teacher, to the person it expresses
> and to the purposes it articulates. Failure to understand the teacher's voice is
> failure to understand the teacher's teaching. (Hargreaves, 1994 p.249)

What does it mean to be a teacher today? In chapter one we briefly explored the changing face of education in Britain and the impact this is having on our notions of teacher professionalism. This short discussion highlighted the complex developments that teachers must continually respond to, and the competing and often confusing policy demands they are required to negotiate. Meeting the benchmarks of the standards agenda whilst implementing inclusion is no simple matter within the context of the broad and exhausting remit that awaits teachers when they walk into their classrooms every morning. The reality is that whilst teachers think about how to turn policy into practice, there are still registers to take, jotters to be marked, paperwork to be completed, meetings to attend, classrooms to be organised and pupils to be taught. And then there are pupils like Malcolm...

In chapter one it was suggested that teaching in British primary schools has, until fairly recently, been predicated upon a range of notions about children and learning that have their roots in the Piagetian developmental model. This model is characterised by a particular set of constructions about children and their capacities, with an emphasis on children's inherent vulnerability and need for protection, and reference to fixed stages of cognitive development linked to age and readiness. Age stereotyping continues to structure constructions of childhood today and profoundly influences the way that adults listen to and control children within educational contexts (Lee, 2001). The

idea that adults have an unproblematic right to control children is deeply embedded in our cultural psyche, and is often treated uncritically within educational discourse. However, the evidence of cross-cultural studies challenges
the idea of age hierarchies and taken-for-granted notions of authority and
control (*ibid*). These themes are also contested within the emerging children's
rights literature (Sinclair Taylor, 2000).

Confusingly, however, tensions over teacher authority and the role of pupils'
rights are being played out within the context of a market model of schooling
(Tomlinson, 1997). This market model values competition, rewards and sanctions, hierarchical structures, and the language of the market place. In
England and Wales, and to a lesser degree Scotland, this market model priori-
tises the delivery of a culturally defined curriculum incorporating ascribed
levels of attainment and measurements of pupil achievement. These priorities have, of necessity, skewed and defined the central aims of teaching and
learning and have shaped an educational culture in which children's personal
knowledge and versions of reality have been treated as marginal, if not
irrelevant.

This educational paradigm has served to justify and amplify the teacher roles
of protection and provision at the expense of pupil participation. It has also
served to entrench children's structural position, within both the education
system and society as a whole, as the 'invisible group par excellence'
(Qvortrup, 1990, p81). It should now be clear that, in the context outlined
above, the notion of primary pupils as individuals who can be self-aware, self-
reflective and capable of communicating their subjective experiences is
bound to be a contentious one. It seems to fly in the face of accepted norms.
Further, the idea that children's contributions should be actively listened to
and taken seriously is still more alien. These notions are frequently embedded in the ethos of primary schools. This is the air that many primary
school teachers breathe.

Considered optimistically, it might be argued that legislative developments
on children's rights, and the introduction of inclusive policy and practice, are
set to transform this educational context profoundly over the coming years.
Teachers are currently being urged to set traditional constructions of childhood aside, transform their role, and engage with the diversity of pupil
perspectives in the classroom, especially where there are additional support
needs such as persistent disengagement. Traditional values and practices
have therefore come into direct competition with those of the inclusive ideal.
It is not unreasonable to presume that as the impact of inclusion gathers

pace, the notion of pupil participation in educational decision-making will slowly begin to gain credence at classroom level.

But we are not there yet. It remains to be seen whether the participatory principle at the heart of inclusive practice is merely 'a passing fashion' or a 'foundation for a new order of experience' (Fielding and Rudduck, 2002, p2). If the latter proves to be the case, there is no doubt that the journey towards this new order will be a long and difficult one for many teachers, especially those who have been in the profession for many years.

Let us now explore the reasons for this by listening more closely to the teachers in the Sommerville study. Their perspectives are considered within the context of the wider research so that it is possible to grasp the universality of their concerns. What emerges is the complex reality of the teachers' predicament when confronted by persistent disengagement and under-achievement. An understanding of this lived reality will help to put teacher responses into perspective and explain why, when pushed to the limit, they may default to behaviours that I have labelled survival strategies. Teacher survival strategies are explored below and added to the interactive model of disengagement and intervention introduced in chapter three.

The Sommerville study: teacher perceptions of, and response to, disengagement

According to social constructivist thinking, teachers' understandings about pupil learning, behaviour, teaching and discipline are first formed through personal experience of attending school and learning about schooling within the family and the socio-culture context beyond. This deeply personal knowledge and experience is developed and transformed through the processes of higher education and teacher training, and refined via the potent subjective experience of classroom teaching itself. Thus, though teacher perspectives are highly individualised, certain areas of knowledge known as 'professional craft knowledge' (Brown and McIntyre, 1993, p17) are likely to be shared, at least to some extent, by those who participate in the process of 'becoming a teacher'. This taken-for-granted knowledge carries the blueprint to which teachers refer when making sense of, and addressing, pupil learning and behaviour in the classroom.

Teacher perceptions amongst the Sommerville cohort reflected aspects of this shared blueprint. When these perceptions were analysed further, it became clear that teacher response is strongly influenced by two important, practical purposes:

> **Purpose 1**: to stop pupil disengagement and get pupils back to learning
>
> **Purpose 2**: to intervene in a way that is sensitive to specific context and self factors

Purpose one might be viewed as teachers' primary concern and must be fulfilled in order for teachers to meet their most important and pressing professional obligation – to get pupils through the curriculum whilst ensuring academic progress and achievement. Interventions to stop disengagement are based on two factors identified by the Sommerville teachers:

- their personal perceptions of pupil behaviour
- their personal style of pupil behaviour management

This primary teacher purpose can only be fulfilled by achieving some sort of balance between context factors such as time and workload, and underlying self factors such as teacher beliefs and feeling states. Teacher intervention might therefore be construed as a set of compromise responses aimed at resolving the tension between these primary and secondary purposes. Let us consider each one in turn.

Purpose 1: Stopping pupil disengagement

Teacher perceptions of pupil behaviour

In the Sommerville study, teacher perceptions of pupil disengagement suggested that certain behavioural acts had more salience for teachers than others. For example, talking was the behaviour most frequently commented upon. Playing and wandering around were also of some significance. This is a common finding in the research on teacher perspectives (Munn *et al*, 2004). Researchers highlight the fact that the behaviours that teachers find most problematic tend to be relatively trivial – it is the sheer relentlessness of these behaviours that teachers find stressful. Low level pupil indiscipline is number one in the 'top ten sources of stress' identified in a recent comprehensive study of teacher health and wellbeing (Dunlop *et al*, 2004).

Interestingly, the surface behaviours the teachers found salient did not always correspond to those highlighted by the pupils themselves. For example, 'trying to be good' was a category of significance to two pupils in the cohort, and refers to instances where they felt that they were making a deliberate effort to work hard to meet teacher expectations. These pupils complained that their teachers failed to notice their efforts. Two pupils also emphasised acts such as name-calling and throwing things around the classroom. Again, their teachers did not mention these behaviours. And there were several instances where teachers associated pupil disengagement with talking, whilst the pupils themselves associated it with a completely different sort of behaviour such as daydreaming. Perhaps most striking, however, was the salience given by pupils to feeling states compared to their general lack of salience for most of the teachers in the cohort.

These varying patterns of salience highlight the fact that there is often no consensus between pupils and teachers upon the nature of an individual pupil's disengagement. This illuminates the existence of what I have termed 'perception gaps' – a generic label connoting the apparent invisibility of certain acts, states and happenings to individuals that seems to delimit their subjective field of perception. The teacher perception gap associated with pupil name-calling and throwing acts may be quite easily explained by pupil efforts at concealment. Pupil instances of 'being good', on the other hand, may well have been noticed by teachers but considered irrelevant to a discussion of disengagement. But it is less immediately obvious why a teacher should find pupil talking salient, whilst the pupil in question focuses on daydreaming. Nor is it clear why pupil feeling states should fall into teacher perception gaps.

A possible explanation might be derived from the work of Goleman (1997). Drawing on the work of sociologist Erving Goffman (1959), Goleman suggests that people's definition of the situation (i.e. their construction of reality) to some extent underpins what they pay attention to and how they interpret the world. Echoing social constructivist thinking, Goleman suggests that this definition of the situation has both a personal and a shared dimension. It is highly personal in the sense that it is influenced by an individual's accumulated subjective knowledge and experience of how the world is. However, Goleman emphasises that this knowledge and experience can be skewed by psychological events that create blind spots, or what he terms 'lacunae', in personal constructions. He defines these lacunae as:

> ...defensive gaps in awareness ... [or] ... black holes of the mind [that] divert attention from select bits of subjective reality – specifically, certain anxiety provoking information. (*ibid,* p107)

Goleman goes on to explain that subjective definitions of the situation can also be shared because they are influenced by collective definitions or 'frames':

> A frame is the shared definition of a situation that organises and governs social events and our involvement in them. A frame, for example, is the

understanding that we are at play, or that 'this is a sales call', or that 'we are dating'. Each of those definitions of social events determines what is appropriate to the moment and what is not; what is to be noticed and what ignored; what, in short, the going reality involves. (*ibid*, p197)

All frames therefore have what Goleman terms a 'dual track':

...one flow of activity is overt and acknowledged, while a parallel track is ignored, treated as though out of the frame. Anything out of the frame, by definition, does not deserve attention. (*ibid*, p201)

In Goleman's terms, then, the concept of perception gaps is synonymous with the perceptual zone that lies 'out of the frame'. When applied to a classroom context, his thesis implies that teachers' definitions of pupil behaviour might be construed as arising from both their personal definition of the situation plus shared notions or frames regarding, for example, what learning is, what disengagement is, plus notions of teacher and pupil role, etc. Thus, if as the findings indicate, talking is construed by teachers to be a key act of disengagement, then, according to Goleman's thesis, this might be linked, on the personal level, to the fact that learning is associated by some teachers with expectations of a quiet, stress-free classroom and silent, focused pupils, closely correlated to personal tolerances for noise. An individual with low tolerance for noise might be especially sensitised to pupil talk.

On a shared level, the salience of talk might also be amplified by the fact that 'not talking' is a ubiquitous and potent school rule in British schools. Further, an atmosphere of 'quiet busyness' is a common and shared yardstick for assessing pupil behaviour and, perhaps more significantly, teacher control. According to Goleman, low levels of talk might be viewed as a significant item within the 'collective frame' relating to both good teaching and good behaviour.

In practical terms, the salience of talk may also simply relate to the fact that a busy teacher can hear talking without looking up, whereas daydreaming or throwing acts need direct visual attention before they become apparent. As a corollary, even if a pupil is daydreaming fairly regularly, the teacher may, for the reasons above, pay more attention to talk. For such a teacher, daydreaming will fall into a perception gap.

The lack of salience of pupil feeling states for several teachers in this study might also be explained using Goleman's framework. It is conceivable, for example, that some teachers may not feel personally equipped to deal with negative pupil feeling states. On the personal level, some individuals might have developed the 'defensive lacunae' that Goleman postulates exist to protect us from 'anxiety-provoking information' (*ibid*, p107). For example, the knowledge that pupils can feel some considerable hatred for certain teachers may be exactly the sort of information that teachers might, understandably, want to protect themselves from.

Perception gaps regarding pupil feeling states may also be reinforced by the fact that teacher expectations in Britain tend to be predicated upon, and shaped by, the assumption that learning is a dispassionate cognitive activity (Donaldson, 1992), and that classrooms are not the context for emotional sharing except under teacher controlled conditions such as Circle Time (Hanko, 2003). Thus teachers may not accept that dealing with negative pupil feeling states comes under their professional remit. If this is the case, it should not be surprising that pupil feeling states have low salience for such teachers and lie outside their professional frames.

In the Sommerville study, such teacher perception gaps were continually reinforced because the teachers did not attempt to explore pupil points of view. Mrs Parker was the exception, since she made a conscious attempt to gather pupil perceptions and to address pupil concerns by directly involving them. The rest of the teachers in the study, however, were rarely confronted with, or challenged by, pupil perceptions. As a result, they may have lacked the insight that their perceptions were partial. This point warrants strong emphasis, given the widespread cultural acceptance of teacher definitions of disengagement as the only legitimate basis for teacher intervention.

Goleman's theoretical framework therefore appears to have some explanatory power. It yields useful insights into the discrepancies between teacher and pupil perspectives and offers support for the notion of perception gaps. It also sits well within the social constructivist paradigm. However, it is extremely difficult to verify Goleman's theory. His thesis is supported by a plethora of research that would have to be closely scrutinised in order to reach any convincing judgment. Most of it lies outside the fields of knowledge relevant to this book and would call for an excursion into unknown territory. Acceptance of his framework should therefore be considered tentative.

Teacher explanations for disengagement

Teacher explanations for pupil behaviour are also distinct from pupil explanations in that they focus largely, though not exclusively, on pupil self factors rather than context factors, especially deficit explanations such as attitude or temperament faults, and dysfunctional family background. Thus teachers highlight individual and family pathologies as key causal attributes. The research indicates that this is a common finding (Blease, 1995, Watkins and Wagner, 2000, Araujo, 2005).

However, two teachers, Mrs Parker and Mrs Edwards, acknowledged that their own behaviour might have had some impact on pupil behaviour. Mrs Edwards, for instance, expressed concern that her 'confrontational' approach to disengagement might have exacerbated Edward's attitude of defiance and escalated his behaviour. Mrs Parker, on the other hand, was convinced that her efforts to establish a warm and trusting relationship with her pupils, and involve them in discussions and interventions had a positive impact on both behaviour and achievement. The rest of the teachers in the cohort did not mention this possibility, either with regard to themselves or with regard to teachers in general. Nor did they discuss the possible impact of other context factors, such as the curriculum, on pupil behaviour.

There is a large body of literature (e.g. Charlton and David, 1993, Slee, 1995, Macrae *et al*, 2003) that takes as its premise the idea that the context of learning is highly significant, if not decisive, in the genesis of disengaged behaviour. This literature refers repeatedly to the importance of theorising the institutional factors, such as teacher behaviour and the curriculum, that affect pupil behaviour and performance. It also emphasises the difficulty of achieving this in an outcomes driven policy context where blaming and excluding pupils may be considered more efficacious than working with pupils to enhance quality of provision.

The fact that the teachers in the Sommerville study emphasise pupil self factors rather than context factors may also reflect an 'understandable reluctance' (Charlton and David, 1993 p24) to face the possibility that they might be partly responsible for pupil underachievement. Upton (1993) adds that it is rare for any attempt to be made in classrooms to explore systematically the influence of teachers on pupil behaviour. He emphasises that teachers, as a group, are as prone to emotional and psychological distress as any other grouping, and may, in some cases, be unable to respond to pupil needs appropriately as a result.

Thus teachers as well as pupils may 'participate in the social construction of certain forms of deviance' (*ibid*, p113). Taken together, teacher and pupil perspectives suggest that an array of context and self factors are likely to underpin the aetiology of pupil disengagement. Some of these factors appear to be more clearly recognised by pupils; others are more clearly recognised by teachers. This suggests a more complex picture than is generally acknowledged in the literature, where the debate tends to be polarised. School effectiveness literature traditionally emphasises in-school context factors, whereas the psychological literature emphasises pupil deficits and family background. The important point that arises from the Sommerville study is that there needs to be some acknowledgement and synthesis of both sets of perceptions.

Interestingly, neither pupil nor teacher perceptions highlight class, race or gender as causal influences underpinning disengagement, though there is a body of evidence that suggests that these are key factors (McFadden and Munns, 2002). Much of this research evidence is based on issue-led, rather than perceptions-led, methodologies that proceed from the *a priori* assumption that class, race and gender are unquestionably integral to disengagement. Methodological differences may therefore account, at least in part, for the discrepancy. For example, it would be surprising if a study of pupil perceptions revealed that young pupils used highly abstract and rather sophisticated concepts like gender to explain their classroom behaviour. But the reasons why teachers did not refer to these factors are less clear. One can only assume they had no salience for the teachers in relation to this particular pupil cohort.

In summary, then, the discussion above clarifies how teacher response to pupil disengagement is predicated upon their subjective perceptions of pupil behaviour. What becomes quite clear is that most of the teachers in this study perceive pupil surface behaviour in a distinctive way, focusing in particular on pupil talk. Yet they do not perceive many of the dimensions pertinent to the pupils themselves. The roots of pupil disengagement are considered, by all the teachers in the cohort, to lie at least in part in the pupils themselves, or in the influence of their home background. However, two teachers do concede that teacher behaviour has some influence. Given this set of assumptions, it is not surprising that the majority of the teachers in the cohort focus their behaviour interventions almost exclusively upon challenging and changing pupil behaviour, and not on questioning context factors such as teacher response or the role of the curriculum.

Teacher perceptions of behaviour management

In the Sommerville study, pupil, teacher and parent perceptions indicated that teacher behaviour management responses could be organised into three distinct categories. The 'negotiatory' response was characterised as pupil-centred and was typified by the priority given to the development of a trusting and secure relationship with pupils, the involvement of pupils – and parents

– in negotiations about learning and behaviour, and pupil collaboration in behaviour interventions. The 'confrontational' response was conceived of as the diametric opposite of the above. It was characterised as teacher-centred and authoritarian, and associated with the use of extrinsic behaviour change systems involving sanctions, such as verbal reprimands, removal from the classroom, detentions and report cards, and rewards such as praise, stickers and star charts. The underlying aim of the confrontational response was pupil conformity. The 'flexible/tactical' response, on the other hand, was viewed as a synthesis of the two. Teachers showing this response used negotiatory approaches such as dialoguing and pupil involvement, but also drew on extrinsic behavioural interventions associated with the confrontational style according to what worked best with individual pupils. Two teachers in the Sommerville cohort self-categorised as mainly negotiatory; two self-categorised as mainly confrontational; and one teacher self-categorised as flexible/tactical.

A review of the literature indicates that the range of approaches set out above are fairly typical of how classroom teachers deal with the low-level disruption caused by disengagement (Pollard, 1985, Merrett and Jones, 1994, Hanko, 1994). Pollard's (1985) work in primary classrooms, based on pupil and teacher perceptions, has made a valuable contribution to this body of knowledge. Pollard suggests that teacher responses to pupil learning and behaviour can be categorised into four broad groups. He distinguishes between the strategies of open negotiation, domination, routinisation and manipulation. The first two categories have much in common with the negotiatory and confrontational responses that emerged in the Sommerville study. Though the remaining two categories did not specifically arise, it is interesting to note that routinisation and manipulation are not dissimilar to the flexible/tactical response in that they fall between the other two more opposed categories of teacher behaviour, and draw approaches from both. Pollard's work therefore supports the main thrust of the Sommerville findings.

However, whilst teacher self-perceptions tell us how they believe they respond to pupil learning and behaviour and how they self-categorise, pupil perceptions of teacher behaviour can add another dimension to the emerging picture of teacher response. Significantly, the Sommerville findings indicated clearly that pupil perceptions did not necessarily match teacher perceptions. For example, pupils felt that teachers were more confrontational than the teachers themselves did. In particular, pupils drew attention to the distinction between teachers who were shouters and those who were non-shouters but teachers did not make this distinction at all. This finding was discussed with reference to the relevant research literature in the previous chapter but an explanation has to be sought for why pupil and teacher perspectives were at such odds in this area.

One explanation, already explored in some detail, is that certain teacher behaviours may fall into a teacher perception gap. For example, teacher shouting is not associated with cultural notions of the 'good' teacher. So it might be difficult for teachers to admit that shouting is a feature of their classroom repertoire. Alternatively, raising the voice may, for some individuals, be a learnt and habitual response to stress which is highly taken-for-granted and invisible to them on a personal level. These two levels may then interact. Thus, a taken-for-granted, unconscious, shouting response may be driven further out of an individual's perceptual frame by the threat of professional guilt and anxiety.

Note that this explanatory model might be applied to pupils as well as teachers. For example, it is equally conceivable that a pupil's perceptions of teacher response might be driven by underlying cultural expectations of teacher role – teachers always shout – and personal defensive mechanisms – shouting makes me anxious. These underlying schemata might lead to a situation where pupil attention is selectively attracted to shouting responses whilst more negotiatory responses fall into a perception gap. Thus, it becomes difficult for the pupil to judge teacher response accurately.

This is a purely hypothetical explanation, based on Goleman's (1997) theoretical framework. Other explanations should also be borne in mind. The disjunction between teacher self-perceptions and pupil perceptions of shouting may be a semantic anomaly linked to pupil meanings. For example, it is possible that shouting may be a catch-all term used by pupils for the forceful application of teacher power that does not necessarily have to include the raising of the voice. On the other hand, for teachers the term may have a more literal meaning. Teachers' apparent failure to speak of shouting may also simply arise from some weakness in the Sommerville research methodology that prevented the issue from coming to light. For example, the face-to-face nature of teacher interviews may have proved too pressurised and unsafe for such disclosures.

Whatever the explanation, the fact that teacher self-perceptions are rarely challenged by competing pupil perceptions, especially in formal ways that teachers would be obliged to consider, may well serve to ensure that teacher perception gaps regarding their own behaviour are perpetuated and become more robust over time. This has serious implications for pupils. It consolidates the asymmetry of power that is a central feature of pupil/teacher relations, and ensures that pupils remain vulnerable to teacher responses that might exacerbate their difficulties. In the worst-case scenario, pupils could be exposed to harmful and unprofessional teacher behaviour, rare though this may be.

Purpose 2: Accommodating context and self factors

The findings of the Sommerville study indicated that several teachers were aware of a number of context and self factors that actually constrained, if not undermined, their primary purpose i.e. they effectively prevented them from stopping pupil disengagement and reversing academic underachievement.

Context factors

Three out of the five teachers in the study complained that their behaviour management options for dealing with disengaging pupils were severely limited by context factors. In particular, teachers mentioned that a lack of time, attributed to the pressure of increased workloads and large class sizes pushed them into quick-fix responses that tended to be somewhat confrontational in style.

For example, one teacher, Mrs Mitchell, felt that Simon, a disengaging pupil in her class would actually benefit from a 'one-to-one teaching situation' for some of the school day in order to avert 'explosive situations'. She added; 'I don't physically have the time to sit with Simon all the time, much as I would like to. It's just not physically possible with twenty-nine other children in the class.' The Sommerville teachers thus acknowledged that they ended up managing and containing behaviour rather than dealing with underlying pupil problems. This is a common criticism of behaviourist approaches to indiscipline (Watkins and Wagner, 2000).

These teachers emphasised that their ideal would be to spend more time with disengaging pupils and approach difficulties in a more pupil-centred, negotiatory fashion. Mrs Parker, a highly negotiatory teacher, confirmed that her approach could initially be time-consuming and required 'extra work', though she pointed out that it tends to save time in the long run. She acknowledged that she could not blame teachers for choosing other options.

Hargreaves (1994) associates this problem of work load with the increase in 'bureaucratic control and standardisation' in contemporary education, and an associated preoccupation with productivity, administration, financial efficiency, and standards of achievement (p113). He suggests that the result has been an enormous 'intensification' of teachers' work (p117) leading to 'pressure, stress, lack of time to relax and lack of time even to talk to colleagues' (p136). This has been confirmed by a number of researchers (e.g.Woods *et al*, 1997; Ball, 2004).

The issue of class size and its effects on teacher and pupil performance is much talked about amongst teachers (GTC, 2005), in the literature, and in the public domain. According to Blatchford and Martin (1998), however, it is an issue that is actually rather 'uninformed' by educational research (p132). They suggest that this is mainly because studies of the causal links between class size and performance indicators are extremely difficult to design. Nonetheless, their review of the research lends support for the contention that large class size has a deleterious effect on 'teacher morale, stress and enthusiasm' (p131). In the light of the findings of a more recent study, Blatchford (2003) concluded that smaller class sizes can enhance 'quality of teaching', increase the likelihood of pupil involvement and reduce 'inattentiveness and off-task behaviour' (p165). It thus reflects the views of the teachers in this study.

Self factors

Two teachers in the cohort also talked in some detail about the self factors that can influence teacher responses to pupil behaviour. Both teachers specified how underlying beliefs and opinions inform teacher actions and may have consequences, both positive and negative, for pupil learning and behaviour.

Mrs Parker, for example, based her teaching upon a deeply felt belief in the importance of warm and trusting teacher/pupil relations, and the notion that pupil disengagement is usually linked to low self-esteem. These underlying beliefs informed her pupil-centred, negotiatory response to disengagement in the classroom, but worked, she felt, to the benefit of all pupils. Mrs Edwards, by contrast, emphasised that her confrontational style was linked to her personal belief in 'fairly firm discipline', pupil 'conformity', and the importance of 'not making allowances' for troublesome children. She believed that a tight rule system in the classroom was the only way of stopping things from 'falling apart'. She noted, however, that all teachers have their own style of behaviour management, and believed it to be a 'highly personal thing'. Mrs Edwards acknowledged that her approach may have exacerbated the problems she was having with two disengaging pupils in her classroom, and said she was trying some negotiatory tactics to see if they helped. However, she confessed to finding this shift of style 'very difficult'.

Some teachers also acknowledged that pupil behaviour had an impact on their feeling state, and suggested that this could have consequences for teacher response. For example, some teachers reported feelings of frustration and anger as a result of having to deal repeatedly with disengaging pupils. These teachers did not indicate whether they expressed these emotions to pupils by shouting, though pupil perceptions clearly suggested that some did. Two teachers said they attempted to put their feelings aside and deliberately adopt a calm or neutral feeling tone in front of pupils. This is a fairly common way for teachers to handle their emotions (Dewe, 1985).

These personal and idiosyncratic dimensions of teacher action are of growing interest to educational researchers. They are the underlying subjective realities that come into play when there are sustained problems of pupil behaviour in the classroom. Goodson (1992) suggests that over the last two decades there has been a gradual shift away from the study of teacher role towards the study of teacher biography, teacher voice, and the underlying motives that influence individual teacher practice, as a means of penetrating the exact nature of underlying subjective realities. He, like Mrs Edwards, believes that teaching is 'intensely personal' (p234), and suggests that when researchers listen to teachers talking about their lives as practitioners they find that their 'professional practices are embedded in wider life concerns' (p16).

Butt *et al* (1992) and Hyman (1990) both point out that one of the most important justifications for listening to teacher perceptions is that they can shed light on the reasons why the idiosyncrasies that define individual teacher style are so robust and enduring in the face of classroom research advocating alternative styles and approaches. For example, Hyman questions why, despite the widespread dissemination of research into the effectiveness and efficacy of preventative and positive approaches to behaviour management, some teachers still do not make use of them. He feels that the answer lies in the 'lack of attention to the powerful aetiological factors which most determine teachers' responses' (Hyman, 1990, p109). He suggests that many teachers pursue confrontational behaviour management strategies because they hold the underlying belief that 'fear of punishment is the best motivator' (p110). He proposes that teachers' childhoods may play a significant role in the development of such beliefs and quotes a number of studies that have established a strong correlation between adult punitiveness and experiences of punishment in early life.

Pollard (1985) proposes a similar theory. On the basis of his qualitative study of teachers and pupils in primary classrooms, Pollard suggests that teacher behaviour is predicated on powerful biographical factors that underpin teacher 'self-image'. Like Hyman, he suggests that childhood experiences are significant to teacher response, as are age, gender, social class, race. He also identifies teacher 'workload', and 'health and stress' as two key teacher 'interests-at-hand' that teachers must accommodate in their classroom lives (*ibid*). His findings therefore reflect some of the self and context factors highlighted in the Sommerville study.

Pollard goes on to suggest that teacher attempts to fulfil their professional duties whilst accommodating these interests at hand will be achieved in highly individualised ways. However he claims that the teacher strategies he calls open negotiation, dominion, routinisation, and manipulation can all be viewed as prototypical strategies commonly found in primary classrooms. Pollard refers to them as 'coping strategies' (p155) i.e. adaptive approaches that enable teachers to cope whilst also protecting their sense of self.

The Sommerville teachers: coping or surviving?
Though the concept of coping strategies may well be apposite for the broad cohort in Pollard's study, this notion does not seem to apply in the context of the Sommerville study. This may not be surprising, given the nature of the teacher and pupil sample, and the focus on disengagement. The findings indicate, for example, that two teachers in the cohort felt that they were simply 'containing' their pupils without addressing the real reasons for their underachievement. One teacher, as we have seen, felt that her own responses might be making pupil behaviour worse. Four out of the five teachers in the cohort felt that their strategies were simply not effective in dealing with the pupil behaviours under consideration. These teacher comments suggest that their current strategies were stretched to the extreme and that they were pursued at some cost:

■ **The effects of intervention were temporary:** Teachers found that their interventions were always circumscribed by context and self factors that continually compromised their efficacy. As a result, intervention only resolved pupil disengagement superficially and temporarily. This inevitably frustrated their primary purpose.

■ **Intervention caused problems:** Because the effects of intervention were temporary, teachers found that they had to repeat them frequently. This heightened emotion, used up time, challenged personal and professional beliefs, and thus exacerbated their secondary purpose i.e. the accommodation of context and self factors. Intervention therefore aggravated a situation that was already difficult. It trapped teachers in a cycle of stress and frustration.

The teachers in the Sommerville study were well aware of these costs. Some took action to deal with them by trying to change their behaviour management strategy e.g. by becoming more negotiatory. However, in doing so, they created further tension for themselves by overriding their personal and professional beliefs and by putting themselves under even more pressure. Other teachers explained that they approached support services for help at this stage. But some of their comments suggested that they became despondent with this solution because input was often superficial or impractical. Mrs Mitchell, for example, acknowledged that she had grown cynical of the possibility of support from the educational psychologist. She commented; 'Oh, I wish! I've yet to see [the educational psychologist] come up with anything concrete. I mean, I shouldn't say this, but I've yet to see him come up with anything concrete and constructive.'

Thus the Sommerville teachers, like their pupils, were actually functioning at a survival, rather than a coping, level. They were simply managing to get themselves and their pupils through the school day, and evidently had a fragile hold on teaching and learning in respect to their disengaging pupils. The notion of teacher survival strategies thus seems a more accurate way of conceptualising teacher response to pupil disengagement in the Sommerville cohort.

The findings showed one significant exception. Mrs Parker's beliefs and behaviour support strategies contrasted sharply with those of the rest of the teachers in the research group. Thus, whilst they directly articulated a subjective sense of not coping, Mrs Parker's comments consistently suggested that she felt positive about her approach with disengaging pupils, and confident that they were benefiting from her input. Pupils and parents directly confirmed this and made it clear that they appreciated her constructive approach to disengagement. It seems likely, then, that Mrs Parker had found a way of coping in the classroom that, as Pollard suggests, enabled her to satisfy her own interests-at-hand whilst at the same time addressing the specific difficulties of her disengaging pupils. Thus she achieved what Pollard labels a 'working consensus' i.e. the 'mutual accommodation' of pupil and teacher definitions of the situation (Pollard, 1987, p178). Pollard suggests that this sort of mutuality is characteristic of the teaching and learning relationship between the majority of teachers and pupils in most primary classrooms.

Mrs Parker appears to have achieved this working consensus by adopting a negotiatory strategy that was an amplified version of her normal classroom style. Thus, whilst she was a teacher who was always at pains to develop a trusting and warm relationship with her class, she seemed to work on this element much more carefully in the case of disengaged pupils. She also went further with them in her attempts to make her practice and expectations transparent, and spent extra time involving them in the analysis of their difficulties and the joint formulation of individualised interventions. Though Mrs Parker acknowledged that this was a time-consuming approach that placed a heavy burden of work upon her in the early stages, she claimed that she was soon able to pass responsibility for learning back to the pupil. This was achieved via the cultivation of pupil reflection and self-regulation that arose as a positive side effect of pupil involvement. For example, Mrs Parker helped pupils to develop skills for independence via the use of pupil diaries and tick lists that enabled them to take responsibility for change. This strategy, when it began to bear fruit, permitted Mrs Parker to delegate intervention to the pupils so that they were effectively monitoring their own behaviour. This reduced the need for continued, intensive teacher input. The hard work of negotiation was therefore temporary, and was offset by growing pupil participation and autonomy.

It seems clear that Mrs Parker's approach had been honed by years of practice and was underpinned by deeply held beliefs about the capacity of young children for such forms of collaboration. She dealt with the problem of workload and pressure of time by working in her lunch hour, and also by ensuring that any intensive input was temporary. Thus, unlike the other teachers in the Sommerville cohort, she did not experience any dissonance between self and context factors, nor between her primary and secondary purposes. Neither did she experience the costs the other teachers encountered. So Mrs Parker might reasonably be described as a teacher who was coping rather than simply surviving. She was an exceptional case, going against the general trend of the findings.

A model of disengagement and intervention

Details of teacher purposes and costs can now be added to the model of disengagement and intervention introduced in chapter three. The resulting model (figure 4 overleaf) illustrates how these purposes and costs underpin teacher intervention and interact with pupil survival strategies.

This model provides a visual representation of the stalemate that disengaging pupils and their teachers can so easily get locked into. This stalemate is the

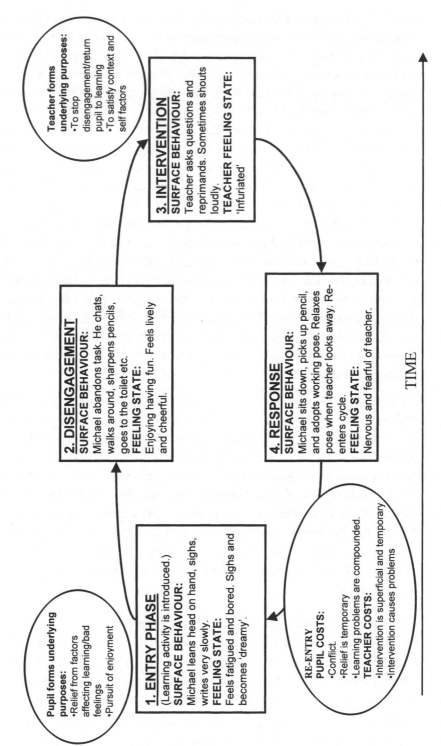

Figure 4: Michael's cycle plus pupil/teacher purposes and costs

hallmark of everyday life in the classroom for these children, and can, unfortunately, be repeated and reinforced again and again over time.

Our discussion so far has suggested that this situation arises, essentially, where there is a significant lack of intersubjectivity or shared understanding of how things are in the classroom, and where things have gone wrong. This is directly linked to unshared perceptions and the resulting multiple perception gaps in teacher knowledge of pupil purposes. This, in turn, generates skewed interactions and shallow forms of intervention that simply serve to exacerbate the situation further. Thus, we end up with a paradoxical situation in which teacher interventions have a detrimental effect on pupil behaviour by reinforcing and amplifying disengagement rather than diminishing or resolving it. None of this happens deliberately nor is it what teachers actually want.

This tendency for teacher intervention to reinforce pupil behaviour is referred to as the 'multiplier effect' (Pollard, 1985, p238). Pollard refers to this in relation to teacher coping strategies, and suggests that teacher coping behaviours will tend to positively reinforce pupil coping behaviours through the processes of interaction and associated processes such as the self-fulfilling prophecy. It is interesting, then, that this multiplier effect also operates where the working consensus has broken down. In this context, teacher survival behaviours seem to negatively reinforce pupil survival strategies through exactly the same processes. Unfortunately in this scenario, the consequences for pupils are far more damaging.

The teacher's predicament: is there a way out?

In the quote at the start of this chapter, Hargreaves suggests that if we provide teachers with an opportunity to articulate their points of view, and then listen to what teachers have to say, we are rewarded with valuable insights into their lived experiences and an understanding of the foundational beliefs and theories that underpin their constructions of their own professional practice. The insights of the teachers in the Sommerville study have clarified how differently they negotiate the complexities of classroom life, and how personal and subjective these negotiations can be. However, the wider research highlighted the universality of many of their concerns. It seems clear that dealing with persistent disengagement and chronic underachievement within a complex, outcomes driven, and pressurised educational context inevitably puts teachers in a stressful predicament. They must somehow meet the conflicting requirements of educational policy on the one hand, whilst on the other, meeting the needs of a class of twenty-five pupils, the specific needs of disengaging pupils plus their own needs as teachers and human beings. Teachers know that they cannot always do a good job in such circumstances. There is no doubt that they generally do the best they can.

There is also little doubt that teachers' response to these pressures and stresses has implications for pupils in the classroom. Our discussion has clarified how the survival strategies that teachers use to deal with disengagement can actually consolidate pupil behaviour and make matters worse. These survival strategies are, I would suggest, an understandable outcome of the convergence of so many urgent and competing demands. No wonder teachers throw their hands up in dismay and feel inclined to get out of the profession.

Yet, the example of Mrs Parker enables us to identify the role that multiple perspectives might play in the development of a practical approach to disengagement in the primary classroom. Her practice suggests that collaboration with pupils is not only possible but can be highly effective in reducing the debilitating effects of disengagement on pupils, and relieving the frustration and stress experienced by teachers. Collaboration with pupils may, therefore, suggest a way out of the teacher's predicament. Potentially, it can enhance shared understanding, diminish perception gaps, and bring teachers and pupils together in a joint endeavour to make better sense of disengagement in the classroom.

Collaboration such as this does not require teachers to follow step by step recipes that will reliably lead them towards a desired set of outcomes. The picture, alas, is rather more complex. There is a growing consensus within the educational research literature that collaborative practice, if it is to achieve meaning and depth, implies a reconstruction of underlying beliefs about teaching, learning and behaviour that will facilitate a transformation of professional practice in the classroom (Head, 2003).

This transformation is not about 'one size fits all' or standardised solutions that focus on changing pupils. It is about pupils, teachers and parents working together to jointly define a problem, to identify its various roots, and to explore solutions that address problems within the pupil/teacher/parent triad and the wider learning environment beyond. I call this way of working an intersubjective approach, for it relies on the development of shared understanding. Yet, in a sense, it is much more than an approach: it implies a particular vision of teaching, learning, and, indeed, schooling. This vision, and the teacher qualities and skills associated with it, are the subject of chapter six.

For the moment, however, a crucial piece of the jigsaw is still missing from our overall understanding of disengagement. The perceptions of parents in the Sommerville study supplies this missing link. In the next chapter we take a step out of the primary classroom to consider what disengagement looks like from a parent's point of view. What do parents see from their vantage point beyond the school gates? Why should teachers consider collaborating with them?

5

'Parents welcome': perceptions from the school gate

...you could shout and scream till the cows come home ... if they weren't interested, they weren't interested... (Crozier, 1999, p322)

G ill Crozier is quoting a mother who believed that the teachers she was dealing with had no intention of really listening to her. Though the example may be extreme, her impassioned words point to the anger and frustration some parents experience as a result of their dealings with teachers and schools, and hint at the complexity underlying glib pronouncements on partnership in the educational debate. Despite pockets of good practice across the primary sector, research repeatedly confirms the existence of an uncomfortable gulf between theory and reality with regard to collaboration with parents (Crozier and Reay, 2005). There is ample evidence to suggest that, whilst parents are welcome in schools, there are often subtle but powerful strings attached to the notion of partnership. When it comes to parental involvement in delicate matters of pupil behaviour and discipline, warm words of welcome can quickly grow cold.

This chapter considers why parent/teacher partnerships are such a thorny issues for many primary schools and explores the many and complex barriers to partnership and collaboration that get in the way of effective communication within the teacher/parent dyad. We start by listening to the Sommerville parents and consider how far their perspectives reflect those apparent in the wider research. Their influence upon our emerging model of disengagement and intervention is examined.

The Sommerville study: parent perceptions

According to social constructivist theory, parent perceptions of pupil disengagement are likely to be related to a number of interacting influences. These might include parents' subjective experiences of once being a primary school pupil, their awareness of cultural attitudes about pupils and their behaviour, their personal perceptions of pupil and teacher roles, and, importantly, their detailed knowledge and understanding of their child. Many of these influences will be highly idiosyncratic, and this accounts for the sheer diversity that characterised parent accounts in the Sommerville cohort. However, certain influences tend to be shared by parents within a school culture and these are reflected in the many commonalities of perception within the parent group field.

Certain recurring themes arose from these parent commonalities. These can best be understood in relation to two key underlying parental purposes that appeared to underpin their perceptions of pupil disengagement:

> **Purpose 1**: to develop a clear picture of their child's disengagement using parental knowledge and understanding
>
> **Purpose 2**: to develop this picture further by making sense of perceptions mediated by pupils and teachers

The central parental purpose was to try to develop a clear picture of their children's disengaged behaviour so that they could support them and help them back to learning. To achieve this, the parents in this cohort drew on an enormous wealth of personal knowledge and understanding of their children's personality, abilities and behaviour, the social and historical context of the children's development, and their observations of their children during homework sessions.

However, since parents were not present in the classroom to directly observe their children's behaviour, parents found that they had to supplement their knowledge and understanding by negotiating a complex set of mediated perceptions – those of their children and the teachers. Making sense of these mediated perceptions therefore constituted their second, related purpose. This purpose was generally complicated by the fact that mediated perceptions were frequently incomplete, divergent or contradictory. Let us consider these two purposes.

Purpose 1: Developing a clear picture: the role of parental knowledge and understanding

Parents obviously have a vast amount of personal knowledge and understanding of their children as individuals. They have the enormous advantage, over teachers, that this knowledge and experience is usually deep, complex, multi-dimensional and under constant review and development. It is based on observations of their children in an array of different social and learning contexts, involving many different people and a variety of different forms of action and interaction. Parents draw on this fund of experience when they are asked, as they were in this study, to discuss the nature of their children's classroom behaviour and performance, and make sense of their disengagement.

Several parents in the Sommerville study explained their children's disengagement with reference to character traits they traced back to very early childhood or even babyhood. John's withdrawn and rather sullen behaviour, Hannah's dependency and dislike of being academically stretched, and Andrew's poor memory and organisational difficulties were all contextualised in this way. This historical perspective also enabled parents to point up discontinuities of behaviour. For instance, Mrs Dobson highlighted the fact that Michael used to be a quick, bright and precocious learner as a young child but was growing increasingly demotivated and apathetic.

Parents also have the advantage of being able to put their children's behaviour into familial context, linking pupil ability and response to specific learning patterns within the family group. For instance, Gary's mother explained her son's easy boredom with learning tasks in light of her own learning responses as a pupil and those of his sister, suggesting that it was something that ran in the family. Edward's mother, on the other hand, made sense of her son's learning behaviour by comparing and contrasting it to the behaviour of his older brother. She linked his learning interests to the early influence of his father's hobbies and enthusiasms.

Parents also highlighted significant relationships and events within children's biographies and related them to behaviour and performance. For example, the birth of siblings, difficulties with peer relationships, illness in the family and changes of school were all considered to be relevant to disengagement in the classroom.

Parent experiences of schooling also appeared to have a bearing on their perceptions. For example, one parent questioned the influence of the teaching methods at Sommerville on her son's learning performance, and reflected upon the value of the rote learning she was exposed to as a child. Another parent suggested that his son's disengagement might improve if he was exposed to a more authoritarian regime in the classroom. He felt he had benefited, in the long run, from strict discipline when he was a pupil.

Against this backdrop, however, parental observations of their children's responses to homework seemed to be particularly influential in the development of their perceptions. Such observations furnished parents with detailed insights into their children's difficulties, and response to them, when faced with formal learning tasks at home. This helped them to build up an impression of their children as pupils.

Levels of parental interest and involvement in homework varied considerably across the parent cohort but all the parents in the Sommerville study made some contribution. On the basis of routine observations of homework behaviour, parents reported problems of motivation, distractibility, cognitive confusion, daydreaming, poor organisation, poor writing posture, and difficulties getting thoughts down on paper. In some instances, these behaviours mirrored those that regularly occurred in the classroom. In other instances, they did not. Parents ultimately depended upon their children for clarification on this matter and, as we relate below, could not always rely on what they heard.

Homework sessions also provided parents with experience in the role of 'parent as teacher', albeit in an informal capacity. This experience appeared to generate insights into the sorts of responses and interactions that might surround their children's learning behaviour in the classroom. For example, some parents described the advice and support they tried to offer during homework, and the opposition they encountered as a result. Simon's parents, for instance, referred to their painstaking efforts to help him get his ideas down on paper. They were hurt and confused when this advice failed to make any difference. Hannah's mother explained how she tried to help her daughter to be more independent with her homework, but found her so stubborn and resistant that she ended up writing much of it for her. Though research on homework is scant in the UK (Hughes and Greenhough, 2003), there is some evidence to support the Sommerville parents' view that it can be a source of tension between pupils and parents (*ibid*). Several parents in the cohort felt able to empathise with their child's class teacher because of their frustrating experiences as teacher in the home.

The perceptions outlined above highlight the underlying personal knowledge and understanding that all the parents in this cohort brought to the process of making sense of pupil disengagement. This broad, multi-dimensional knowledge base may account for the wide range of explanations that parents contributed to discussions of their children's behaviour. It may also explain why parent perceptions did not show the self/context polarisation, or 'attributional bias', that arose so clearly in pupil and teacher accounts.

The value of this sort of parental knowledge, and the contribution it can make to teacher understandings of pupil behaviour and performance, is well established in the educational literature (Vincent, 1996; Crozier and Reay, 2005). The idea of home/school partnership has a very long pedigree within educational discourse, and much of the ongoing enthusiasm for partnership is based on the plethora of research, stimulated many years ago by the Plowden Report (1967), which has repeatedly highlighted the benefits for children, teachers and schools as a whole, of parental involvement in education (Tizard and Hughes, 1984; Cullingford, 1985; Flouri and Buchanan, 2004). This research recognised that parents can act as an essential bridge between home and school, play a vital role in reinforcing school values and norms, and support learning in the home. Thus it is now considered axiomatic that parents are 'welcome in school' and 'seen as potential partners and educators' (Cullingford and Morrison, 1999, p253). This view has recently received a significant push from the top down via legislation to enhance parent power and secure parents' right to direct participation in decisions effecting their children's educational provision.

Contemporary research continues to suggest that parental involvement has clear benefits for pupils in terms of improved attendance, attainment and behaviour (Tett *et al*, 2001). It also has benefits for the parents, bringing enhanced self-esteem, competence and confidence, and valuable insights into the workings of school (*ibid*). There is broad acceptance of the idea that the active and genuine involvement of parents is a dominant feature of schools that are 'successful in promoting positive discipline' (SEED, 2001, p4). Evidence also suggests that teacher/parent partnerships have improved since the 1990s – especially in the primary sector (HMI, 2005).

However, beyond the rhetoric, and despite this generally positive trend, there is accumulating evidence that the lived reality of partnership with parents is far from straightforward (Meighan, 1989; Pollard and Filer, 2003; Crozier and Reay, 2005). In many cases meaningful partnership that rises above a purely functional and superficial level is difficult to achieve. The findings of the Sommerville study suggests that the ambiguity surrounding parental involvement in education might be linked, at least in part, to issues around the 'mediation of perceptions', to which we now turn.

Purpose 2: Developing a clear picture: negotiating mediated perceptions

Parent perceptions are not based on personal knowledge alone but reflect a distinct pattern of commonality or disparity with pupil and teacher perceptions that are directly linked to the process of mediation i.e. to what parents pick up from teachers about their children, and from their children about teachers.

For example, parent and teacher perceptions converged quite unambiguously within the Sommerville study with regard to perceptions of surface behaviour, and also correlated positively to associated evaluations and perceptions of outcome. Teacher discourse about pupil behaviour was mirrored by parent discourse, despite the fact that parents had never observed their children's behaviour in the classroom nor had the opportunity to make direct evaluations. Both parties used terms like 'disruptive', 'distracted' and 'attention seeking' to describe pupil behaviour and associated these behaviours with negative evaluations.

It is likely that these linkages can be traced to the reporting of behaviour that passes between teachers and parents during informal chats, in report cards, and on parent evenings, and which tends to focus on descriptive and evaluative accounts. These reports transmit the values, modes of discourse and interpretations of behaviour that are characteristic of teachers and schools. It should not be surprising, then, that they become highly familiar to parents and are integrated by them. Parents are, after all, repeatedly exposed to this framework throughout their children's school years, and must engage with it, time and again, in order to acquire information about their children's behaviour and performance. When they like and trust individual teachers, parents are likely to presume that, within reasonable limits, the assumptions, judgements and claims made by them are reliable, fair and legitimate (Pollard and Filer, 2003).

However, the Sommerville study clarifies that although teacher claims may well be perfectly fair and justified from teacher points of view, there is a possibility that they could be incomplete and partial in important respects. This is because teachers do not always take pupil perspectives into account when they are examining pupil behaviour and performance and developing their judgements and responses to it. So their commentaries are not always entirely reliable – in some cases, they may be unfair and illegitimate. When teachers pass these perception gaps on to parents, misunderstandings and distortions about pupil behaviour and learning are inevitably compounded and amplified. This happens again when parents, in turn, mediate teacher perspectives back to their children, especially if they fail to redress the imbalance by eliciting their children's self-perceptions and self-evaluations.

Yet this process can work in a similar manner in the opposite direction. In the Sommerville study there were two component areas in which parent and teacher perceptions tended to diverge: perceptions of feeling state and perceptions of teacher response. Here, pupil/parent commonalities were generally more frequent.

For example, five parents in this study were especially concerned that their children's disengagement might be linked in some ways to teacher response, particularly shouting. Parents directly linked their concerns in this area to pupil reports of school incidents and also to parental observation of their children's feeling state and behaviour at home. Two parents noticed, for instance, that their children seemed to be rather frightened of their teachers and that this fear was manifested in their reluctance to go to school. Others linked their children's upset or anger to stories their children told of teacher shouting, labelling or blaming in the classroom. All the parents in the cohort struggled during interview to highlight their efforts to establish the 'facts' of such pupil stories. They wanted to explore how their children's actions might have precipitated the teacher response. This suggests that these parents were aware, on some level, of the possibility that perception gaps might be passed on by their children, causing distortions in their emerging picture of pupil disengagement.

In an effort to clarify the situation and address potential perception gaps, some of the Sommerville parents opted to arrange visits to school in order to talk over specific incidents with the teacher concerned. Others brought matters up at parents' evening or when they had been called in by teachers to discuss pupil 'misbehaviour'. However, five out of the ten parents complained that teachers had, in some instances, dismissed their concerns about teacher response outright. Several parents were clearly perplexed and upset by this as they now faced the impossibility of establishing a clear understanding of what was going in the classroom. Mrs Lane, Mrs Dobson and Mrs Young seemed to be particularly distressed by experiences of this kind. Such dismissals ensured that pupil perception gaps about teacher behaviour could not be checked out. It also meant that parents were impelled, by default, to become advocates on behalf of their children.

It should be remembered that, contrary to parent and pupil perceptions, none of the teachers in the cohort perceived themselves as 'shouters', and few appeared to be aware of pupil feeling states. Note also that several teachers in the cohort explained pupil behaviour in terms of parental influence, and only two acknowledged the possible influence of teacher behaviour. So a picture emerges of a clash of perspectives between parents and teachers. This dynamic is not uncommon and is reported in the wider research literature (e.g. Crozier, 1999; Todd, 2003).

In a context such as this it is hardly surprising that the mediation of perceptions is problematic for parents. The fact that mediated pupil and teacher perceptions are at best partial and at worst conflicting appears to place parents in a difficult position. The parents in this cohort claimed that they tried to negotiate these perceptions in ways that were fair to both parties, but frequently discovered that they were not always in receipt of sufficient information to be able to achieve this effectively. Their picture of what was actually happening in the classroom was consequently obscured. This was a clear source of confusion and frustration.

By contrast, the three sets of parents working with Mrs Parker were able to develop a more holistic picture of their children as learners. This was because the perceptions mediated by the teacher included pupil accounts, and the perceptions mediated by the pupil included teacher accounts. Parents could therefore make better sense of their children's disengagement and were able to help them, albeit indirectly, by supporting a negotiated set of interventions aimed at addressing pupil, teacher AND parent concerns. These interventions were jointly developed and operated at home and at school so as to achieve coherence and continuity. We already know that, from all points of view, this collaborative solution to disengagement had positive outcomes in terms of pupil learning and behaviour. It also alleviated parent stress. But overall, these experiences were exceptional within the parent cohort.

Several researchers confirm that 'parent power' can be seriously restricted by poor liaison between teachers and parents, especially in matters of pupil behaviour and discipline. This is attributed to a climate of mistrust and blame that frequently prevails beneath the rhetoric of partnership (Cullingford and Morrison, 1999; Crozier, 1999). This mistrust is linked to a number of different factors. Jones and Lock (1993) suggest that a mutual lack of insight into parent and teacher 'roles', 'intentions' and 'constraints' (p173) may account for poor partnership and collaboration. They also propose that a poor grasp of the idea that behaviour at home and at school are not necessarily related may have an impact on the development of perceptions. Certainly, the parents and teachers in the Sommerville study did not seem to question this assumption. Other researchers link the blame culture to a clash of values and to the impact of language and power differentials between parents and teachers (Crozier, 1999; Maclure and Walker, 2000).

For example, some parents may perceive teachers as experts and expect them to get on with the job of dealing with behaviour and discipline in the classroom. They may have attitudes of deference and dependency and fail to see what contribution they can make to the partnership. They may not appreciate the constraints on teacher time, and the impact of their child's behaviour on other pupils, yet they expect the teacher to take full responsibility for the resolution of the problem. However, teachers who unquestioningly accept this expert role and expect parents, rather like pupils, to simply agree with them and conform, can reinforce this dependency. At the same time they may complain about it and wonder why parents are reluctant to get involved. They may not appreciate that some parents are intimidated by teacher authority and do not have the confidence to speak up on important matters.

Other parents may be more assertive and feel sufficiently empowered to question teacher points of view – like some of the parents in the Sommerville cohort. Meighan (1989) suggests that parents like this may fail to meet teacher expectations and fulfil the school's criteria of the 'good' parent – i.e. one who is 'well informed or in agreement with the school's ideology' or who 'manages the impression that this is the case' (*ibid*, p107). He argues that parents who fail these criteria are likely to be perceived as threatening and interfering. Munn *et al* (1992) agree and suggest that, despite the rhetoric of parental partnership, 'the reality has more typically been that parents are called upon to support the school's way of doing things' (p104).

For a variety of reasons, then, parents can find it difficult to challenge teachers on their children's behalf over sensitive matters of behaviour. However, this is also a more general trend. For example, a large scale HMI study of parents' satisfaction with schools concluded that schools that do not listen to, or act upon, parental concerns are the source of significantly lower levels of satisfaction (HMI, 2005). Ninety-three parents who participated in this questionnaire study were highly satisfied with their child's primary school and felt that their contributions were valued but 76 judged their primary school to be unsatisfactory or poor by the same criterion (*ibid*, p9).

Tett *et al* (2001) confirm that whilst parents in general find most teachers approachable and appreciate parent evenings as a way of finding out about their child's progress, there is a perception that schools are not 'necessarily communicating the things parents want to know most about' (p54) and 'have few structures in place to listen to parents and to identify their priorities' (p55). There is also evidence that teachers do not provide enough specific guidance for parents to enable them to support their children. As a result, parents cannot always grasp how, exactly, they might play a more meaningful partnership role. Indeed, most parents have minimal direct involvement in their children's formal schooling (Russell and Granville, 2005).

The evidence from the Sommerville study and beyond suggests that there are substantial numbers of parents who still feel that the quality of the home/ school partnership leaves much to be desired. Thus in many instances, the rhetoric of collaboration continues to betray the reality. Teachers reading this book will surely be familiar with the many conflicts and tensions that can undermine the teacher/parent dynamic, for they play themselves out in one form or another again and again in schools across the country. Yet they are not what parents or teachers want and they are certainly not in the best interests of teachers, parents or pupils.

The ongoing problem of poor quality partnership points to the need for a far deeper appreciation of the delicacy and complexity of the issue. Research suggests that schools need to be much more strategic and pro-active in involving and valuing parents, and more willing to address barriers to partnership (Russell and Granville, 2005). Government policy is already heading in this direction. For example, in Scotland, policy makers claim they will 'modernise and strengthen the system for supporting parental involvement in school education' (SEED, 2005, p1). How this will be achieved and whether it will be successful is another matter.

It seems likely that a combination of the factors explored above may have been at play in the Sommerville context and could account for the difficulties highlighted by parents. There is mounting research support for the proposition that parental partnership receives its warmest welcome where there is conformity to teacher points of view and an acceptance of teacher authority. According to Todd (2003):

> A deficit discourse underlies almost every initiative to involve parents; conversely, 'professional practices' are treated as non-problematic. (p281)

Challenging teacher perceptions is bound to be contentious within such a context.

The findings of the Sommerville study suggest that the notion of parental partnership is particularly problematic in contexts where parent, pupil and teacher perceptions conflict, and where underlying perception gaps are not exposed and addressed. Without a remit of open, respectful partnership within the teacher/pupil/parent triangle, which includes the right to challenge teacher perspectives and school ideology, the parents in this cohort found it almost impossible to construct a clear understanding of their children's disengagement and underachievement. The pursuit of parent purposes in this restricted context gave rise to two specific costs:

- **Parents became trapped in the role of piggy-in-the-middle:** Parents found that with teacher perceptions on the one side, and pupil perceptions on the other, they had no effective means of bridging the gap unless teachers were willing to listen to their concerns and answer their questions. Where this did not happen, parents ended up integrating and perpetuating existing pupil and teacher perception gaps with the result that parents themselves became mediators of the *status quo*.

- **Parents encountered conflict with both teachers and pupils:** When parental concerns were side-lined or ignored, this compounded difficulties at home and at school, and triggered further confusion and stress for parents.

To summarise, then, it seems clear that the mediation of perceptions is a subtle but central problematic in the formation of parent perceptions of disengagement. In the Sommerville cohort, as we have seen, parents acted as mediators of teacher perceptions in some areas, and as mediators of pupil perceptions in others. As mediators of teacher perceptions, parents amplified perceptual distortions regarding pupil behaviour by articulating teacher definitions of the situation and perpetuating teacher perception gaps. But this worked both ways. As mediators of pupil perceptions, parents also amplified distortions regarding teacher response by articulating pupil definitions of the situation and perpetuating pupil perception gaps. So it is important to note that, through the process of mediation, parent perceptions can have a powerful, albeit remote and indirect, influence on patterns of disengagement and intervention in the primary classroom. Parent perceptions can potentially fuel both dimensions of the pattern. Pollard's 'multiplier effect' seems to be in operation here.

A model of disengagement and intervention

The underlying purposes and costs set out above can now be added to the model of disengagement and intervention that has evolved over the last two chapters. The updated model (Figure 5 overleaf) indicates that the parental

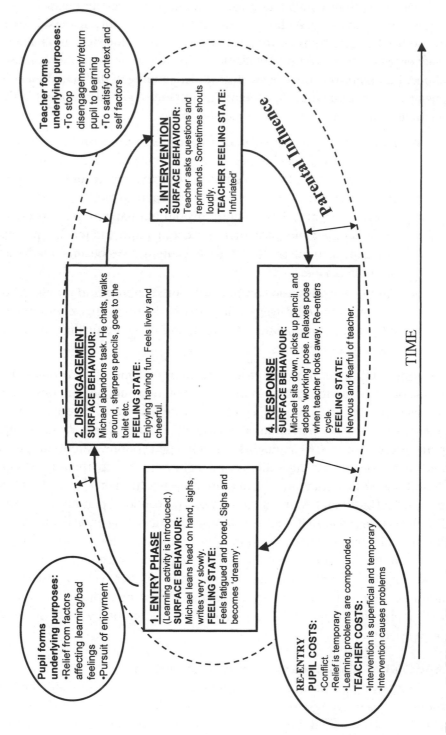

Figure 5: Michael's cycle plus parental influence

influence works by lending background support to teacher and pupil perceptions in some component areas, and perpetuating perception gaps in others. This can obviously fuel the clash between pupils and teachers and actually helps to maintain cycles of disengagement and intervention. This completed model therefore represents the three-way dynamic that underpins classroom disengagement and pinpoints the powerful perceptual forces that energise and drive it.

It should be clear by now that any attempt to halt and reverse the motion of this dynamic in order to reduce disengagement and restore pupil/teacher relations will demand a deep understanding of the interplay within the pupil/teacher/parent triangle. This contention is not simply logical or theoretical but is also based on the practical example provided by Mrs Parker. Her collaboration with pupils and parents illustrates the possibility that patterns of disengagement can be reversed and outcomes enhanced. This possibility is predicated upon a 'deep' definition of partnership (Head, 2003) in which parent perceptions are listened to, negotiated and acted upon, and in which they are invited to become genuine participants in the process of behaviour analysis, solution development and implementation. This issue is explored and developed in the next chapter, where the implications of the Sommerville study are examined in detail.

Before we move on, it is tempting to speculate as to whether or not parents, like pupils and teachers, operate coping strategies or survival strategies. The term coping strategy as applied by Pollard (1985) connotes 'a type of patterned and active adaptation to a situation by which an individual copes' (p155). The term survival strategy, on the other hand, has been coined to define a situation in which pupils and teachers are no longer coping, teaching and learning has broken down or ceased, and where enjoyment and satisfaction have given way to recurring feelings of vulnerability and distress.

Note that the notion of coping is never applied by Pollard to parents and he does not touch upon this in his study of classroom processes. Yet there may be a sense in which the construct applies. For example, it might be argued that the parents in the Sommerville study were involved in 'patterned' and 'adaptive' ways with their children's difficulties over time. Many parents described exactly how their involvement with their child during homework had become a household routine, with specific characteristics, of, for instance, timing, place, organisation and input, and how their liaison with teachers had taken a predictable shape. Their accounts also clarified how their 'interests-at-hand' (Pollard, 1985), or their 'purposes' as I refer to them here, were inextricably linked to the development of these patterns.

It is also clear from their subjective assessments that their involvement with their children's homework was frequently a frustrating and problematic experience for the Sommerville parents. These frustrations recurred in ways that were ultimately linked to the ambiguities of partnership, and the problems this created for interpreting and negotiating mediated perceptions. Parental comments indicated little sense of coping on their part, but were more indicative of a survival level of experience characterised by repetitive but unsuccessful attempts to develop a clear picture of their children's disengagement, and repetitive but unsuccessful interventions, both at home with their children during homework, and at school via negotiations with teachers.

Arguably, the emotional component of the parent's struggle was particularly indicative of survival, with frustration, confusion and upset frequently to the fore. By contrast, the three sets of parents who worked with Mrs Parker recognised that their involvement with their children's learning had been transformed by her openness and collaborative approach. It appears that these parents, after years of struggle, were beginning to experience a sense of coping.

However, the Sommerville study did not focus on parents' experiences in any depth. Parents were not subject to the lengthy and detailed observations that were conducted in classrooms. Further, teachers and pupils were not asked to reflect upon parent input, though it was frequently mentioned in passing. So there is little research data to directly support the notion of parent coping or survival strategies and the contention can only be regarded as speculative. The subject, however, is an intriguing one, and perhaps warrants further research.

Summary
Throughout our discussion of pupil, teacher and parent perceptions over the past three chapters, we have acknowledged the heterogeneity of subjective perceptions and the value of an appreciation of the sheer diversity of pupil, teacher and parent voices in the Sommerville cohort. However, the identification of group fields of perception concentrated our attention upon numerous areas of commonality that were linked to pupil, teacher and parent purposes and their associated costs. The wider research mentioned across this discussion indicates that these common areas of concern are far from idiosyncratic and reflect the experiences of participants in other studies and in other contexts.

Our discussion went on to explore the possibility that the specific acts of disengagement and intervention that habitually arose in the Sommerville classrooms might be construed as pupil and teacher survival strategies. This construct re-framed our understanding of what was going on in these classrooms, and represented a shift away from simplistic polarities such as the 'deviant pupil' versus the 'uncaring teacher' towards a consideration of the pupil and teacher dyad as an interactive, intersubjective system. Behaviour on both sides might be viewed in this system as a somewhat distorted but ultimately rational, human response to a highly complex and powerful set of underlying purposes, pressures and constraints. Again, links to the research literature provided ample support for the existence of these subtle underlying forces in other contexts, suggesting that the findings of the Sommerville study might be confidently generalised to similar populations. But these generalisations are naturalistic rather than scientific, and there are certainly no grounds to claim that the experiences of the Sommerville participants can speak directly for the experiences of other teachers, parents and pupils. However, certain features may ring true for readers who have found themselves in similar circumstances, and may provoke thought, self-reflection and self-evaluation.

The theoretical model introduced in chapter three and completed in this chapter provides a diagrammatic representation of how surface behaviours (the *inter*personal level) and underlying perceptions (the *intra*personal level) work together to reinforce and consolidate pupil disengagement. This was explained in relation to the role of perception gaps, the lack of intersubjectivity between teachers and pupils, and the resulting shallow and short-term nature of teacher interventions. The model was extended to illuminate the potent background influence of parent perceptions in the production and reinforcement of pupil and teacher perceptions, and the way parent perceptions are linked to the processes of mediation and to their role as mediators.

Thus the book has so far illustrated the significance of subjective perceptions for our understanding of pupil disengagement. Perhaps we are at last coming closer to a solution to the conundrum posed in chapter one: how can we begin to reconcile the competing realities that underpin disengagement in the primary classroom? How, in Hargreaves' powerful words, do we make a 'choir from a cacophony' (Hargreaves, 1994, p251)?

It should be clear by now that the solution lies in a participatory approach that is grounded in teacher, pupil and parent perspectives. I call this an intersubjective approach – literally one that brings disparate subjectivities together to develop a joint understanding of disengagement and under-achievement, and a shared vision of how it might be overcome. It should be obvious that the evolution of this intersubjective approach must address the key themes, processes and mechanisms uncovered over the course of the last chapters in order to enhance mutual understanding and sharpen the focus of joint involvement and joint intervention.

If teachers, parents and pupils can come to understand the workings of the specific patterns of disengagement and intervention that are causing problems in the classroom, they will be rewarded with valuable insights that can be transformed into practical solutions. As is so often the case, the seeds of change are inherent within the problem. However, to grasp this demands a dramatic shift of perspective by teachers. It requires that disengagement be viewed as an opportunity to be seized rather than a situation to be dismissed, managed or blamed on pupils and parents. This, in turn, requires that teachers recognise their own potential role in the genesis and reinforcement of classroom disengagement. Much depends on the attitudes of those involved. The leadership of the teacher is clearly pivotal.

In the following chapter the discussion of disengagement takes a more pragmatic turn. Drawing on our analysis so far, we consider the essential features of an intersubjective approach to disengagement in the primary classroom on the basis of what we have learned from the pupils, teachers and parents of Sommerville primary school and the wider research. The intersubjective approach is explored by returning to the story of Malcolm and his teacher, Miss James (chapter one), using their predicament as an illustrative case study. This will show how, in practical terms, intersubjectivity can be enhanced through certain shifts in classroom interaction and communication that will facilitate the development of a three way partnership-based form of practice.

6

Moving forward together: making it possible

If there is anything that we wish to change in our children, we should first examine it and see whether it is not something that could better be changed in ourselves. (C.G. Jung)

There are hundreds of books on behaviour management on the bookshelves. The best of them are very helpful to teachers, providing constructive and positive strategies that can be applied off the shelf in classroom contexts to encourage reluctant learners back to work. But many of these approaches, despite entirely benign intent, are based implicitly on a child deficit model and the belief that the problem of disengagement resides, essentially, within the child. Many focus exclusively on pupil behaviour modification and tinker with this at a superficial level. Such approaches will work for some pupils some of the time. Mostly, however, they enable teachers to temporarily paper over the cracks I alluded to in the opening chapter of this book. They are a quick fix for pupils like Malcolm, getting them to learn what they don't want to learn and behave in ways that are less troublesome and more convenient for teachers and schools (Wilson, 1991).

Yet these cracks have a tendency to re-surface and break through. The reason for this is simple. If we blame pupils for disengagement and try to manage them by treating them as objects to be shaped by adults, then they will simply learn, once again, that their thoughts and opinions are irrelevant and their feelings, invisible. Whenever this happens, whatever was brewing under the surface of their disengagement is likely to start whipping up a storm. We should not be surprised if the outcome is more, not less, trouble in the classroom.

Breaking out of this unhelpful and ineffective model clearly requires a qualitative shift within the interactive, triadic system discussed throughout this book. It requires that teachers, pupils and parents change what they do i.e. they must make a shift at the *level of action* in order to engage more collaboratively and create a more just, egalitarian and democratic mode of participation. The example of Mrs Parker, her pupils and their parents, confirms that this sort of change is possible and can happen, albeit slowly, through the day-to-day experience of genuine collaborative practice.

However, any shift in action inevitably relies upon a far deeper shift at the *level of meaning*. By this I mean that there must be a transformation in the way that teachers, pupils and parents makes sense of, or understand, disengagement and the circumstances surrounding it. Clearly, this shift must be led by the teacher and rests on a sound grasp of the fundamental insight that classroom behaviour does not happen in a vacuum but is situated within an interpersonal classroom context. Thus making sense of disengagement means, in part, making sense of the environmental and relational factors that may be causing or perpetuating disengagement, and implies an acceptance of the possible influence, amongst other things, of the teacher, their teaching and the curriculum.

It is important to repeat that this does not, in any sense, represent an attempt to shift blame from pupils to teachers. Rather, we need to break out of the blame culture entirely and invite pupils and teachers into a genuine, respectful and shared endeavour in which assumptions and judgements are suspended and a safe space created for open, honest dialogue. However, teachers, rightly, need to be convinced that this step is worth taking and, furthermore, need to be supported in taking it. This will depend on school leadership and ethos, and also upon the trajectories of educational policy and legislation. We return to these matters in the final chapter. First, we need to consider what, exactly, change at the level of meaning and action implies, and how, in practical terms, it might be achieved. The case of Malcolm and Miss James (chapter one) is referred to throughout this discussion and used to illustrate the key principles of the intersubjective approach.

Supporting Malcolm: an intersubjective approach to disengagement

When Malcolm playfully stabbed his neighbour with a ruler under the table, he was initiating a powerful cycle of disengagement and intervention that was unique to himself and his teacher, and reinforced, in various subtle ways, by the mediating influence of his parents. This cycle had Malcolm and Miss

James tightly in its grip. It was causing untold damage to teaching and learning and to the delicate relationships within the pupil, teacher and parent triad.

Ordinarily, Miss James would have responded to this incident by taking the ruler from Malcolm's hand and calmly removing him to a quiet and isolated corner of the room to get on with his work. She might also have reminded him that completion of the spelling task before him would enable her to award him a star for his rather tired looking and sparsely populated sticker chart.

This combination of sanction and reward is a classic behaviour management tactic that will be familiar to teachers everywhere. It is by no means wrong, and is often effective. However, persistent disengagers tend to be immune to it. A gold star, no matter how much it glitters, would be unlikely to motivate Malcolm. Nor would he be troubled by removal to the corner. Indeed, the edge of a room is always a good position from which to survey the lie of the land and keep an eye on the teacher. It is a great place from which to plan the next move.

What, then, might Miss James do instead? How could the intersubjective approach enable her to penetrate this situation and put an end to the relentless cycle that has entrapped them all? In order to answer this question the two levels of change that are characteristic of the intersubjective approach must first be explained.

Change at the level of meaning
Chapter three introduced the idea of the cyclical model of disengagement and intervention. This model provides a visual and conceptual representation of the interactive process at the heart of classroom disengagement that directs our attention towards the behaviour of the teacher as well as the behaviour of the pupil, and clarifies how the underlying perceptions and surface behaviours of both parties constantly feed the interactive dynamic and drive cycles of disengagement forward.

The inclusion of the teacher in this model is a vital and distinguishing feature. It is beneficial in a number of ways:

- it enables us to place disengagement within an intersubjective framework rather than the traditional child-deficit framework
- it establishes the idea of the teacher and pupil as partners in a two-way process based on the sharing of underlying meanings and understandings rather than the uncorroborated beliefs, assumptions and judgements of the teacher alone

■ it directs us to a collaborative solution involving joint working, joint decision-making and joint responsibility, rather than a management solution involving power over the child and the enforcement of extrinsic control

We have already acknowledged that this intersubjective model will present a serious challenge to many teachers. This is because it contradicts traditional conceptions of teacher professionalism and flies in the face of the widely accepted and taken for granted notion that disengagement is a straightforward disciplinary issue that is entirely disconnected from teachers and teaching (Head, 2005).

Turning this sort of thinking around is bound to be difficult. Much will depend, therefore, on the will and motivation of teachers to question their current practice and notions of behaviour and discipline, and their determination to challenge the way they ordinarily make sense of classroom disengagement. This is what we mean by 'change at the level of meaning'. But why should teachers bother with this at all?

The immediate trigger for change in any context might be labelled 'dissonance'. Dissonance arises when there is a conflict of some kind that generates a climate of acute tension and disharmony. This may be an inner or an outer tension – or both – but it is always a highly uncomfortable and bewildering place to find oneself in, and it is generally very difficult to ignore. In the classroom context, the experience of dissonance is readily created by the reality of persistent disengagement and chronic underachievement linked, in no small measure, to levels of stress that some teachers find intolerable. Dissonance, in such circumstances, can therefore act as a trigger that propels teachers to embark on a search for a different and more effective way of dealing with disengagement.

Several teachers in the Sommerville study seemed to be in the throes of this process. For example, dissonance caused Mrs Edwards to begin to question her underlying belief in the necessity for pupil conformity and the efficacy of her avowedly authoritarian approach to pupil disengagement. She even speculated that it might actually be making matters worse. Her next step was to consider experimenting with a more pupil-centred, negotiatory approach, though she confessed that this was uncomfortable for her, contrary to her beliefs and completely alien to her established habits.

These reflections remind us that teacher behaviour, like pupil behaviour, is deeply rooted in underlying perceptions. Though we may not be entirely aware of it, everything we do taps into a vast reservoir of past knowledge and experience with important linkages to an array of idiosyncratic biological, biographical and socio-cultural influences, and to a matrix of underlying values, beliefs, opinions and attitudes that all inform the teacher we become. However, these perceptions are not fixed and static. Rather, they are constantly shifting in response to feedback from the environment. They are also amenable to a more conscious and directed form of change.

So if teachers wish to initiate conscious, directed change within the interactive teacher/pupil dyad, the first step is to reflect upon, identify and question the underlying array of factors that influence our perceptions. This deliberate, reflective effort will enable them to identify their personal style and the strengths and weaknesses associated with it, and will create a firm bedrock for self-understanding and self-development. This self-critical process is the essence of 'reflective practice' – a term that is now well established within the education lexicon. Given its prominence in the literature, and relevance to change within an intersubjective approach, some further explanation of the concept is appropriate.

The reflective practitioner and change at the level of meaning

The concept of reflective practice has its roots in the early work of educationalist John Dewey (1933) who made a distinction between habitual, taken-for-granted 'routine action' and more self-aware, consciously driven 'reflective action'. He defined reflective thinking as:

> Active, persistent and careful consideration of any belief or supposed form of knowledge in the light of the grounds that support it and the further conclusion to which it tends' (in Zay, 1999, p198)

Many educational researchers over several decades have set out to develop Dewey's ideas on reflective thinking (e.g. Schon, 1983; Carr and Kemmis, 1986; Elliot, 1991; MacLure, 1993; Pollard, 2005) and they have all, in various ways, explored the workings of the process. It is generally construed as both a cognitive and an emotional activity (Hinett, 2003) and, simply put, it involves three different stages:

1. **Scanning**: the internal monitoring and identification of underlying perceptions – our beliefs, values, feelings and understandings
2. **Bridging**: the process of stepping out of what is known and habitual by actively questioning perceptions, considering alternative perspectives, making links and combining ideas in order to generate new ways of making sense

3. **Transforming**: using the outcomes of reflection to initiate change at the level of action (based on Silcock 1994).

There is broad agreement that reflective thinking as set out above is a valuable skill for the classroom practitioner. The concept of the reflective teacher is one of the fundamental principles of initial teacher education and CPD (continuing professional development). It is also a recurring theme within educational research and government policy (DfEE, 2001; DfES, 2003d; QAA, 2000; SEED, 2002). Reflective practice is highly valued for a number of reasons.

- it promotes self-awareness and self-control
- it fosters a capacity for mature, dispassionate professional judgement.
- it enables teachers to become active and autonomous inquirers and innovators
- it empowers teachers to take ownership of their own professional development.

The notion of ownership is an important facet of this rationale, and is based on the idea that change will be 'better accommodated ... if it resonates with the hopes, fears and circumstances of the individuals involved' (Maclure, 1993, p312) rather than being imported as an add-on that does not connect with personal perspectives and purposes.

The reflective practitioner is therefore a teacher who:

> ... constantly questions his or her own aims and actions, monitors practice and outcomes, and considers the short term and long term effects on the child. (Pollard and Tann, 1987, p5)

This understanding of teacher role clearly stands in sharp contrast to the traditional view described in chapter one where teachers operate as unquestioning, passive but dogmatic transmitters of received knowledge and belief, and have little awareness of, or concern for, their influence on children and their behaviour beyond the intended outcomes anticipated in their planning. The unreflective teacher can be susceptible to active denial of their influence on pupils, and to the unconscious projection, often onto the 'Malcolms' in the classroom, of their unwanted feelings and behaviours. Such teachers will struggle to achieve an honest understanding of the workings of pupil/teacher interaction as they have not yet achieved a sound grasp of their own intrapsychic workings and underlying perceptions. As a result, they are unlikely to be able to see the need for, let alone create, a safe and accepting context in which meanings can be shared without defensiveness and recourse to blame.

It is not difficult to see that the intersubjective approach sits comfortably within the reflective practitioner framework and has much to gain from it. Specifically, the process of reflective thinking will enable teachers to:

- become more aware of the contents of their 'field of perception' in respect to pupil disengagement
- identify their survival strategies
- acknowledge the specific perceptions gaps that are stopping them from recognising dimensions of the problem that may be important to pupils and parents.

The insights gained from focused reflection upon these matters will pave the way towards increased awareness, openness, sensitivity and flexibility, and will also help teachers progress towards an acceptance of the challenging idea that their subjective perceptions are not necessarily synonymous with the 'truth' or 'reality'. Teachers will then begin to grasp the futility of the 'view from nowhere' (chapter 2) and open themselves up to the multiple realities of the primary classroom. In other words, through the experience of reflection upon the circumstances of disengagement, teachers will be better equipped to take the shift at the level of meaning that must predicate action towards a more collaborative form of working.

The literature on the reflective practitioner (e.g. Pollard, 2005) confirms the insuperable link between the personal and the professional advanced in this book, and suggests that deep and enduring change in the classroom is certainly possible and can be systematically cultivated. Success, however, depends on the quality of the questions we ask ourselves and on how well we observe and monitor ourselves in action. These twin capacities are the essential ingredients of reflective self-awareness and must be practiced and refined until they become embedded in professional practice. This point about embedding is critical, for reflective practice must be an ongoing habit across professional practice, not just a sporadic exercise that is superficial and selective.

What practical implications does all this have for teachers like Miss James? How, exactly, should she put theory into practice?

Theory into practice: reflective thinking and the transformation of meaning

First of all, the process of getting to know what makes us tick as teachers is not an undertaking that can be completed in a session or a day (Pollard, 2005). Reflective thinking becomes easier and deepens with practice and some of us will have had more experience of it than others. Paradoxically, however, the more experienced we are, the more obvious it becomes that the journey of the reflective practitioner has no final destination. There is no point at which it is possible to say that the reflecting can end because we know all there is to know about teaching, learning and behaviour in the classroom! Thus, however far Miss James has come in this respect, the dissonance generated by Malcolm's disengagement will continue to be beneficially addressed by deliberately initiating a process of self-reflection. Though there is no single right way of doing this, she might be advised to begin the process as follows, using structured observation to monitor surface behaviour, and reflective thinking to scan and bridge internal processes.

Structured observation

The cyclical model of disengagement and intervention maps out the interactive landscape in which teachers and pupils, like Miss James and Malcolm, repeatedly meet and clash. The model, reproduced opposite, may therefore be used as a schematic, structured framework for the observation of this four-step cycle, and would enable Miss James to begin to identify Malcolm's unique pattern of disengagement, and her own responses to it, from the moment of entry into the cycle at the presentation of a learning stimulus.

Structured observation is a familiar tool for assessing and monitoring pupil performance in the primary classroom and is not difficult for teachers to carry out. It is likely to yield immediate and valuable insights and information, especially if it is used over a number of cycles so that any recurring patterns of behaviour and response can emerge. For example, Miss James would begin to see how Malcolm settles down fairly well when given an active learning experience, but that more persistent and serious forms of disengagement occur when he is presented with formal paper and pencil tasks like copying spellings or extended writing. This might give her a clue as to how she could tackle the problem via a reconsideration of the curriculum and her pedagogical style.

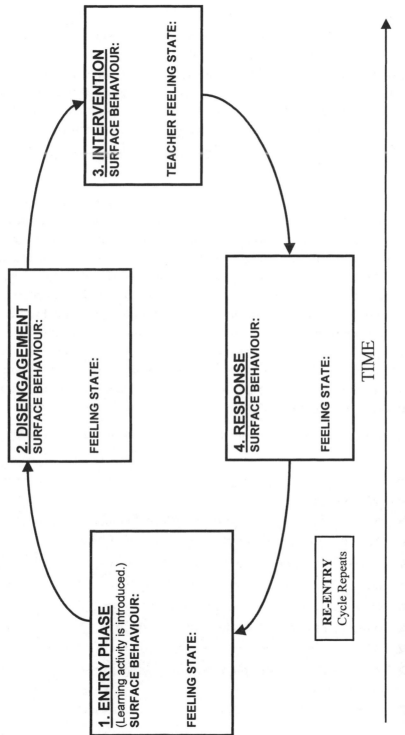

Figure 6: Cycle of disengagement and intervention

Scanning

Miss James might proceed by continuing to deal with Malcolm exactly as usual, but with the proviso that she internally monitor precisely what she is doing and saying, how she is doing and saying it, and what feelings arise within her during her interactions with Malcolm. She must also notice how Malcolm, in turn, responds to her interactions. She might try to find a moment to write down what she has noticed so that she can return to reflect upon it later. Keeping a reflective diary might be helpful.

Bridging

When Miss James returns to her notes, she might try to generate questions about her own behaviour and responses, and also Malcolm's behaviours as revealed by structured observation. In order to do this effectively, she will have to be prepared to ask some penetrating and searching questions that, ordinarily, she might side-step or never even consider. The aim of this self-questioning is not to make Miss James feel bad, induce guilt or apportion blame. Rather, it is to access and make explicit the underlying field of perception that is informing her current responses so that it can be opened up for scrutiny and evaluation. This will enable Miss James to identify potential perception gaps, make it possible for alternative points of view to be considered, especially Malcolm's and his parents', and for alternative responses and solutions to be explored.

Miss James might ask herself some of the questions under the following headings:

> **Questions for self:**
> - Why do I feel so angry with Malcolm when...?
> - Why did I want to reject/punish/ignore him when...?
> - How do I feel when I do that? Why?
> - What is my purpose in doing this?
> - Why do I believe that it is so important to do it?
> - Where do these beliefs/attitudes come from?
> - What would happen if I were to do something different?
> - Is there anything stopping me from trying something different? What is it?
> - Is the curriculum causing problems? How, exactly?

Questions for self continued:

- Is my teaching causing problems? How, exactly?
- What could I do to address these matters in a way that might benefit Malcolm – and others like him?

Questions about Malcolm:

- How would I feel if I were in Malcolm's shoes?
- What is he trying to tell me that I find difficult to hear?
- If I were Malcolm, what would I need my teacher to do to help me?
- Is it possible to try this? If not, why not?
- Why have I never asked Malcolm for his point of view?
- How could I capitalise more on Malcolm's strengths, interests and talents?
- What might Malcolm tell me about the curriculum / my teaching?
- What is stopping me from asking him today ?

Questions about parents

- What are Malcolm's parents feeling?
- What are Malcolm's parents trying to tell me that I don't want to hear?
- Can I be honest with Malcolm's parents?
- Why do I find this difficult?
- Why do I believe that I must be the 'expert'? Can I change this belief?
- Can I admit that I am stuck or stressed?
- What would happen if I ask for their suggestions and listen to them?
- If I was in their shoes, what would I want the teacher to do and say?
- Do I trust them to support this process?
- If not, how can I begin to create this trust?

These questions are intended as suggestions only. Naturally, it is important that Miss James generate questions appropriate to her own situation, as no two instances of disengagement, even within the same classroom, are likely to be the same.

When Miss James adopts this positive, proactive approach, she will no longer be positioning herself as the disillusioned and disempowered victim of pupil behaviour, dependent on the use of formulas to make Malcolm behave. By taking these initial steps, she will begin to experience herself as an active, confident, questioning professional who has a willingness to tolerate the uncertainty that this self-analysis might generate, and the confidence to understand that it is a necessary precondition to change.

However, Miss James needs to know that these critical first steps *must* lead to further steps towards change at the level of action, for the conundrum of pupil disengagement clearly cannot be solved by teacher reflection alone. Thus, whilst Miss James continues to develop and embed her reflective practice, let us consider where she might go from here in terms of directly addressing the factors that are feeding disengagement and causing so much distress in the classroom. This means involving Malcolm in a dialogue with the aim of exploring, and sharing, perceptions of disengagement. We also consider how Malcolm's parents might be invited into the collaborative process and so complete the triadic partnership essential to the intersubjective approach.

Change at the level of action

In order to avoid the view from nowhere discussed in chapter 2, Miss James must be prepared to check out her observations and reflections by engaging in some dialogue with Malcolm and his parents. She must also be willing to act upon their views where appropriate, and involve them in discussions about possible solutions.

This will demand time. The Sommerville teachers highlighted the problem that they have little time to spare during the school day to sit down with pupils and parents to discuss disengagement. This is undoubtedly an important issue for teachers and it is not one we should overlook. Mrs Parker, in the Sommerville study, dealt with it by making use of morning break, the dinner hour and periods before and after school to spend time with her disengaging pupils and their parents. This was her choice and she acknowledged that other teachers might not feel inclined to follow suit. But she emphasised that this input should be seen as a short-term investment that enables pupils, with the correct guidance and support, ultimately to become more self-aware, and to self-regulate and self-monitor their learning and behaviour. Thus, the initial sacrifice of time eventually leads to the transfer of teacher organisation and control, and to more autonomous, more engaged and happier pupils.

We return to the issue of teacher time in chapter 7. For the moment, Miss James and any other teacher confronted with persistent disengagement will obviously have to come to their own conclusions and consider where they might find the time for collaboration with pupils and parents. It is worth bearing in mind that it is only necessary for a tiny minority of pupils in the primary years, and will generally involve only one or two pupils in any single classroom. And think about the teacher time that disengagement is already absorbing with no constructive outcome. By harnessing time positively, Miss James and Malcolm can begin to move on. They must begin to talk and listen to each other.

Exploring pupil and parent perceptions

The Sommerville study and other research studies referred to in this book all provide evidence for the claim that it is possible for young children to participate in discussions about their perceptions. However, such discussions involve the mental manipulation of complex, abstract and, possibly, deeply buried ideas. All these studies emphasise the fact that they must be approached using accessible methodologies within a relaxed, safe and friendly 'enabling' context. Let us examine these guiding principles in order to clarify their meaning and explore how Miss James might attempt to apply them.

Creating a safe space

Teachers, one assumes, are always working within an ethical framework in the primary classroom in the sense that they now have a duty or obligation under children's rights legislation to:

- make provision for the needs of all pupils
- protect them from harm
- ensure their participation in matters of direct concern to them.

(Alderson, 2004 p98).

These principles permeate school life to such a degree that they are generally taken for granted and, thankfully, observed as a matter course. But the meaning of these principles tends to change over time and will also vary from one context to the next depending on how they are interpreted. This is especially true when it comes to pupil participation. Reflective practitioners, like Miss James, must therefore be aware of their personal interpretation, and ensure that there is coherence between their intentions at the level of action and the way that these intentions are carried out. It makes little sense to ensure participation in matters of concern to pupils by using only teacher-centred, teacher-directed approaches, for instance, or by limiting the degree of pupil participation to a level that effectively makes little difference to outcomes. Teachers are advised to avoid such obvious tokenism and to think carefully about how participation is approached.

For example, it will be important that Miss James explains the purpose of the collaborative dialogue with Malcolm and seeks his agreement to take part in their joint venture, just as she would do if she were working with an adult. She must not assume that he will necessarily want to discuss the matter just because she has asked him to. That sort of assumption is not a good basis for open communication and participation. She must also be aware of the need to treat his contributions with respect, acceptance and confidentiality, and assure him that she will not divulge any details of his thoughts and feeling to others unless he wants her to. This is important to help Malcolm feel safe to explore his perceptions with her and assured that he will not get into trouble by doing so.

Many of these ethical gestures come naturally to us when we are dealing with other adults. They are simply considered polite. But they do not necessarily come so readily to mind when we are dealing with pupils who we are used to controlling and disciplining. Unless we are aware of the impact of our power over pupils during these collaborative discussions, they will not be collaborative at all. The discussion will simply dissolve into a teacher controlled exercise in which the pupil feels constrained to anticipate and provide the answers the teachers wants. This could effectively silence Malcolm or arouse his anger and induce further conflict.

Miss James must therefore ensure that she does not use her power and authority as a teacher to manipulate the discussion by asking leading questions, speaking over Malcolm, speaking for Malcolm, imposing her view or by ignoring or contradicting contributions that she finds challenging or difficult to take. The idea, rather, is that she tries to actively listen to what Malcolm has to say and accept it respectfully, *even if she does not agree with it*. This situation is very likely to arise! Indeed, it might be construed as a healthy sign that Malcolm is being honest and feels safe enough to truly express himself. It will also be important that Miss James model this sort of honesty and openness herself, to show that it is expected and allowed, and so that Malcolm can follow her lead.

All the principles mentioned above also pertain to creating a safe space for collaboration with parents. Establishing mutually respectful and ethical boundaries are an important consideration for everyone involved.

Accessible methodologies

Some teachers will be happy to collaborate with pupils and parents quite intuitively. They will feel confident that, on the basis of their knowledge of the pupil, their expertise and experience, they can simply sit down and have a chat together about what is happening when disengagement takes place, and what might be done about it. Others, like Mrs Parker in the Sommerville study, will feel inclined to structure and organise the encounters and draw on their expertise to devise suitable activities to support pupil/parent involvement. Mrs Parker used a range of strategies to this end:

- she devised simple questionnaires for pupils and parents with the aim of gathering basic information about their perceptions of disengagement – including their feelings – and possible solutions to difficulties they identified
- she engaged pupils and parents in developing and designing specific interventions to address problems in the classroom. For example, when she discovered that the main problem for one of her pupils was remembering instructions and getting organised for learning, they got together to create checklists and tick sheets that would enable him take control of his learning and give him more responsibility for helping himself
- she devised a parent and pupil feedback sheet so that they could communicate their thoughts and feelings on a day-to-day basis, highlight what solutions were working well and identify areas for further development

These ideas are extremely simple and easy to operationalise. Yet they set in motion a three-way collaborative process that addressed multiple perspectives, took these perspectives seriously, and ensured that all parties felt valued and involved. This is the essence of the intersubjective approach.

Structuring the collaborative process has the advantage of ensuring that specific issues are explored with sufficient rigour to make the collaborative experience useful and worthwhile to teacher, pupil and parent. It also avoids repetition and will ensure that time, which is at such a premium, is not needlessly wasted. However, it can also lead teachers into a subtle form of agenda setting that enables them to retain control of the collaborative process and direct it in ways they consider preferable. This may act against the interests of pupils and parents, and reproduce inequalities. So it is important that structure is complemented by flexibility and is responsive to the contributions of all parties.

Whether teachers use a structured approach or work in a more informal manner, the underlying aim of the collaborative process will be the same:

- to explore pupil, teacher and parent perceptions
- to identify and address perception gaps
- to problem-solve together
- to develop joint solutions

The following key questions may helpful:

Key questions for pupils:

- Do you enjoy school? If not, why not?
- What are your favourite subjects/least favourite subjects? Why?
- I notice that sometimes you don't really get on with your work – would you agree with that?
- Can you tell me what is happening at such times – describe what you do and how you feel?
- Why do you do this/feel this way?
- Is this a good way to respond? Why?/ Why not?
- Is there anything I do that you find difficult? Explain what and why.
- What can I do to help?
- Can I tell you my point of view (even though we might not always agree with each other)?
- Is there anything we can change together? What could I do?/ What could you do?
- How can we make that happen?
- Which of our ideas will work best? What might stop them from working?

This is a list of reflective questions for pupils that will elicit their descriptions of, explanations for and evaluations of their disengagement, whilst communicating the teacher's desire to collaborate in a non-judgemental, respectful and open manner. However, as all teachers know, some pupils are more verbal than others. Miss James will know that Malcolm is the sort of pupil who finds it difficult to sit still for lengthy periods, and will find it tiresome to have to articulate his thoughts verbally. She would be wise to anticipate this and might consider engaging him in the collaborative experience in more appropriate ways that meet his individual needs.

Ways will need to be devised to gather Malcolm's perceptions of his responses to learning. He might respond positively to a drawing activity that invites him to create a picture of himself doing something he likes in the classroom, and another in which he is doing something he doesn't like. He might use thought bubbles to show what he is thinking or saying during each contrasting activity, and a smiley rating scale to evaluate his experience of it. This will give Malcolm an opportunity to communicate his perceptions visually, without any loss of control or ownership. His drawings and his explanations for the differences between them are likely to be highly illuminating and will provide a useful basis for further activities.

During the Sommerville study, I tried to facilitate, or enable, pupil participation by making use of a wide variety of activities that involved stories, picture stimuli, drawing and video feedback. All of them provided a concrete, stage appropriate and also entertaining basis for the discussion of pupil disengagement that relieved the pupils of the burden of too much talk. Most pupils will quickly tire of being interrogated! So I would encourage teachers to experiment with the ways and means by which pupil perceptions might be explored so that the experience can be accessible and mutually enjoyable as well as fruitful.

Collaborating with parents

Discussions with parents are likely to be less problematic than discussions with pupils because they can be based on a straightforward 'sit down and talk' type format. There is not the same requirement to make them fun and motivating, though it is always helpful to make meetings as pleasant and enjoyable as possible for everyone. However, some considerations are relevant to collaboration with both parents and pupils. For example, though Malcolm's parents may not have difficulties with verbal expression, some parents may need support in this area, for instance if their English is not fluent, or if they feel they cannot put their ideas across. There are various ways of overcoming such barriers e.g. by inviting a translator, or a parent advocate who can accurately represent their point of view. Teachers will have to be pro-active and committed to finding practical solutions to such barriers, and they should take care to actively involve parents in the decision-making and arrangements.

Further, if discussions with parents are to be truly collaborative in spirit, it will be important to signal this by creating a context that is welcoming and con-genial to open communication. The location of the meeting and the organisa-tion of the room will have a powerful influence on the outcome, for these details establish the underlying power relations that are likely to be played out during interaction.

A meeting in the headteacher's office with the teacher sitting behind the desk, for example, is unlikely to convince parents that they will be treated as equals and are safe to share their innermost feelings! A meeting in which the teacher sets the agenda, talks over the heads of the parents and makes all the de-cisions is, likewise, going to defeat the object. Thought needs to go into the organisation of such collaborative encounters to ensure that power issues, language differentials, cultural assumptions and the other subtle factors that can undermine parental involvement will not conspire to subvert the pur-pose of the meeting. (These factors were explored in detail in chapter five.) Needless to say, the ethical factors set out above must also be carefully con-sidered and observed during discussions with parents – especially those per-taining to confidentiality.

Collaboration between teachers and parents will have the same general aims as those identified for teachers and pupils. The following key questions for parents may be useful:

Key questions for parents:
- Do you think your child is happy with their learning? If not, why not?
- What do you think about their disengaged behaviour?
- How do you feel about it?
- How would you explain it?
- What factors in the classroom may be influencing pupil be-haviour? E.g. is the curriculum problematic? What about my teaching/my relationship with your child?

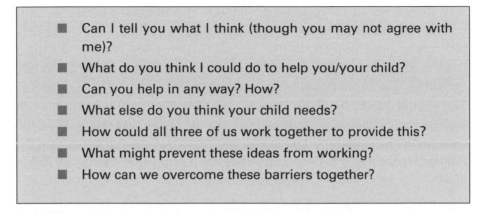

Again, these reflective, open-ended questions are just starting points to stimulate discussion. They will require a sensitive response and careful follow-up. However, some of these questions may elicit feedback that is difficult and challenging for teachers. Some responses could arouse teacher emotions and trigger a desire to stop the conversation, put up a strong defence or launch into an angry counter-attack. Such reactions are human and understandable and may even be reasonable in some circumstances – especially if parents become aggressive or abusive. But it always helps if teachers can control their reaction and deal with clashes in a calm, adult way so that the encounter is not sabotaged or the partnership undermined. This would simply drag the process back to square one and could be damaging for everyone.

If teachers can listen to reasonable criticism, even when they do not agree with it, it will send out a powerful message to parents that their perceptions are allowed and that their right to express them is an entitlement built into the partnership. This fundamental gesture, though difficult and uncomfortable, is likely to generate respect, create trust, and take the partnership on to a new level. It also provides a mature model for parents, and pupils, that may help them, should they need it, to cope with constructive criticism – something most of us have difficulty dealing with.

We must also bear in mind that challenging feedback, whether we like it or not, may actually uncover teacher perception gaps and help to clarify why the situation in the classroom has become so stuck. Information of this sort fulfils a central purpose of the collaboration, and could help to precipitate a real breakthrough at the level of meaning and action.

Having shared perceptions, identified perceptions gaps, engaged in joint problem-solving and explored joint solutions, Miss James will now need to take further action to implement solutions and monitor and review outcomes. The spirit of inclusive, collaborative practice must continue to underpin this ongoing process so that transformation takes place in all three corners of the triadic relationship. Remember, it is not just Malcolm or any other disengaging pupil who must bear the burden of adaptation and change. The central argument of this book is that all parties tend to contribute in varying degrees to the creation and perpetuation of disengagement. Thus, the solution lies in the genuine and meaningful participation of all partners in the intersubjective process. Deep and lasting change must be the responsibility of all.

Solutions, in Malcolm's case, might take the form of specific changes to aspects of the curriculum to capitalise on his strengths and interests. It might also help to address his learning style and preference for more active learning tasks and visual input. Macolm might also need help to resist the temptation to play with rulers and other classroom equipment. He might be motivated, here, by regular, short periods of time out that give him some legitimate space to play across the school day in ways that are negotiated and acceptable to all e.g. being allowed five minutes on the computer. Opportunities to share feelings and explore ways of handling negative feeling states might also be helpful for Malcolm at school and at home. Many of these ideas could well be beneficial for other pupils and will help to ameliorate teacher concerns about preferential treatment.

From survival to coping

Miss James and Malcolm do not want to have to struggle and fight through every single minute of the school day. Malcolm's parents do not want to feel exasperated and isolated. Yet, where there is confusion and misunderstanding, judgement and blame, human beings take refuge in whatever ways are open to them. The resulting survival strategies may seem irrational to the outsider's eye. However, as discussed, they serve an important function in protecting underlying pupil, teacher and parent purposes when faced with persistent failure, overwhelming feelings and stress

Thus, on the face of it, pupils like Malcolm may well appear 'naughty'; teachers like Miss James may well appear 'uncaring'; and parents like Malcolm's may well seem 'difficult'. However, a penetrating look below the surface of their behaviour will expose the logic of their actions and attitudes and enable us to begin to make sense of the meaning of individual responses. It will also give us some vital clues as to how we might begin to transform the situation to the benefit of all.

The journey from survival to coping is therefore a process rather than a recipe. It is a joint undertaking that requires a commitment to the concept of partnership and a realistic investment of time and energy.

Change, however, is never easy.

Miss James clearly has a great deal to think about if she is to follow the tenets of this chapter and begin to explore an intersubjective approach to Malcolm's disengagement. Instinctively, it might seem quicker, and certainly easier, if she were to simply follow her habit and take him off to the corner of the class-room for his daily period of isolation. However, if we re-read the opening section of this book, we will quickly be reminded of the dead end this would inevitably lead Miss James into, and the distressing impact it would have on everyone.

Such recourse is simply not sustainable. It is likely to result in continued deterioration of the pupil/teacher/parent relationship and may have a deleterious effect on health and well-being. It can also culminate in some form of pupil exclusion further down the line – often at secondary level where disengagement is generally less well tolerated. Primary pupils who began as disengagers often become secondary pupils who are completely alienated and disaffected from school. Many young people in this predicament even-tually find themselves removed from mainstream contexts and placed in special units for pupils with behaviour difficulties. Here, if they are lucky, they may come across teachers who will give them a fair hearing and support them in finding constructive ways of dealing with school and learning. Those who are not so lucky may never find their way out of the maze of problems that began, in Malcolm's case, with a relatively innocent penchant for ruler fights under the table.

Surely, this sort of escalation is best avoided? It seems obvious that the sooner in a pupil's school career that the situation is taken in hand the better for all concerned. It also seems obvious that primary class teachers are in a prime position to initiate such a process. I hope, therefore, that the framework set out in this chapter will provide primary practitioners with a map for them to use to begin this journey. The pay-off, at the very minimum, will be a deeper understanding of our pupils and ourselves as teachers and human beings – highly significant rewards in themselves. And if things go well, the intersub-jective approach will enable teachers to gradually transform their relation-ship with disengaging pupils and their parents, and enhance each pupil's capacity to trust, relax, participate, question, experiment, evaluate and trans-form what is happening to them in the classroom.

Notice that this process involves the sort of learning about learning that is of benefit to us all and fosters independence, autonomy and self-regulation. Mrs Parker was keen to emphasise that this was a rather unexpected outcome of the collaborative process she initiated. The other important outcomes were a gradual improvement in engagement, performance and achievement – and happy, informed and proud parents.

Importantly, this intersubjective framework, like any map, is necessarily a somewhat simplified conceptualisation of the terrain to be travelled. It will not, it cannot, prepare teachers for the lived experience of the journey or the unexpected turns it might take. Everyone is different. Thus, every teacher, pupil and parent will react in their own utterly unique way to the processes set out in this chapter. So teachers must be prepared to recognise, accept and engage with these differences with poise and equanimity, and develop a realistic appreciation of the uncertainty that genuine collaboration inevitably involves.

The intersubjective approach comes with no guarantees of a happy ending. Unfortunately, the fruits of teacher reflection and action can never be certain where their focus is human behaviour and the means democratic and collaborative. For when we choose to ask pupils and parents for their cooperation and involvement rather than telling them what to do and dictating the terms, we open the proceedings up to multiple realities and entertain the possibility of multiple outcomes. We are no longer in full control. This means that the nature of the outcome of the intersubjective process will always be uncertain. Yet, paradoxically, it is only by relinquishing control that shared responsibility can flourish, and it is only by sharing responsibility that we optimise the conditions for mutual benefit and change.

The table opposite is a reminder of the differences between the intersubjective approach and the traditional model that currently dominates primary practice. When we are ticking some boxes in the right hand column, we will know that we are on the way to a more inclusive classroom and to a more reflective, collaborative approach to disengagement.

The final chapter explores the implications of the intersubjective approach for teacher professionalism and for pupils and parents. It examines the personal, professional and institutional factors that can impede or enhance the success of this model, and considers the wider cultural and political influences that might affect its future.

Traditional approach	Intersubjective approach
Child deficit model	Child centred model
Teacher controlled	Collaborative
Hierarchical	Democratic
Didactic	Interpretive
Power – over	Power – with
Focus on behaviour	Focus on meanings
Goal orientated	Solution orientated
Superficial	Deep
Unquestioning	Reflective
Management focus	Partnership focus
Teacher responsibility	Joint responsibility
Teacher ownership	Joint ownership
Rigid/one-sided	Flexible/responsive
Social control	Social justice
Conformity	Compromise

7
Are we listening?

...contemporary teacher professionalism needs to incorporate the expectation that teacher learning is both enabled and enhanced by dialogic encounters with their students. (Fielding, 2001 p130)

The central contention of this book is that the daily grind of persistent disengagement in the primary classroom cannot be resolved by patching over old habits and practices with new recipes. Something far deeper and more fundamental is required, that relies for its success on the instinct of the primary teacher to reach out to pupils in difficulty and distress with a heartfelt desire to understand, and a deep belief in the possibility of change. These are the instincts that initially bring people into the teaching profession and without which it would be impossible to sustain one's commitment and enthusiasm for work in the classroom. These same instincts need to be mobilised when we are confronted with challenging disengagers so that, despite our stress and irritation, we can turn back towards them and start listening to what they have to say.

The research described in this book provides evidence that, given a safe and enabling context, young pupils can be specific, constructive and often surprisingly eloquent in communicating their perceptions of their disengagement. They can also be passionate in the expression of their feelings about their school, their teachers and their personal experiences. Likewise, parents, have the potential to contribute a great deal to this debate, not least because of their deep understanding of their child but also because of their invaluable role in bridging the gap between home and school. But they, too, need to feel that the partnership on offer is genuine. When their children are unhappy and in trouble, they may not wish to defer to experts or toe the school line.

Teachers have a choice: they can either continue to exclude and effectively silence the voices of pupils and parents and ignore their potential to enrich and illuminate discussions about disengagement; or they can embrace their right to meaningful participation by inviting them to become partners in a three-way intersubjective process. I hope that the evidence rallied throughout this book will persuade teachers of the considerable benefits of the latter. These benefits can be summarised as follows:

Joint learning: Deeply embedded within the intersubjective model is the understanding, articulated in the opening quote of this chapter, that teachers are also learners, and that teaching and learning are 'interdependent' (Fielding, 2001, p130). A management model fails to recognise this. Within a management framework disengagers are split off from teachers and treated as if they were the sole problem. This de-coupling deprives teachers and pupils of their best source of learning – each other. It leaves both parties stranded and ensures nobody wins.

Enhanced relationships: Persistent disengagement tends to fracture pupil/teacher relationships and generally leads to a breakdown in communication and trust. Management approaches tend to reinforce this stalemate. However, teachers adopting an intersubjective approach have an opportunity to heal damaged relationships by initiating a process based on participation and mutual respect. This gesture immediately signals an intention to suspend judgement and engage empathetically. It has the potential to re-connect teachers, pupils and parents.

Joint understanding: The intersubjective approach equips teachers, parents and pupils with accurate and relevant information about disengagement that is not based solely upon teacher or expert definitions of the situation (the view from nowhere), but on the subjective meanings of all parties. This emphasis reduces the distorting influence of perception gaps and secures the implicit ownership of all those involved. Ultimately, it enables teachers to grasp the deeper meaning of pupil disengagement, and teacher response to it, as a survival strategy driven by underlying purposes that deserve sympathetic consideration and shared understanding.

Joint responsibility: Intersubjective practice offers an alternative to the perpetual assertion of teacher power over pupils and has the potential to relieve them of the burden of day-to-day behaviour control – the sort of ongoing teacher 'nagging' that is so wearisome for all concerned. As Mrs Parker observed, encouraging pupils towards joint responsibility for behaviour change can eventually save teacher time and energy. Thus, in the long run, the intersubjective model can help relieve the stress that so frequently undermines morale within the profession.

Focus on feelings: An intersubjective approach opens the door to the emotional dimensions of classroom experience. This contrasts sharply with traditional approaches that tend to delimit the boundaries of legitimate pupil experience to those elements that are observable to, and accepted by, teachers. Via this model a pupil response such as 'fear of the teacher' potentially gains legitimacy that it currently lacks. When pupil feelings are ignored or invisible, they will continue to fuel disengagement. However, when feelings are acknowledged, pupils can begin to learn how to handle them.

Evidence base: The intersubjective approach has a strong evidence base. For example, there is a great deal of research (see chapters three, four and five) to support the contention that learning engagement is maximised, and disengagement reduced, where:

- teachers understand that pupil disengagement has a meaning
- pupils have a positive relationship with their teacher
- pupil voice is respected, listened to and acted upon
- pupils have a sense of ownership of their learning
- learning is personalised and tailored to needs
- parental voice is respected, listened to and acted upon
- parents play an active, positive role in their child's education.

All this research lends credence to the notion of intersubjectivity, and suggests that there is broad acceptance of its basic tenets.

Successful learners: The intersubjective process has enormous value as a learning experience in itself, for it will enable pupils – as well as teachers and parents – to hone skills in reflective thinking, problem solving and communication, and enhance self-awareness, tolerance, empathy and resourcefulness. Above all, pupils will experience a constructive and empowering process of personal change. These skills and experiences are exactly those required for the next generation in our complex, rapidly evolving, global society. And they are directly aligned to the 'four purposes' (SEED, 2004a) and the 'five outcomes' (DfES, 2003b) of learning stipulated in current UK educational policy. These purposes and outcomes express the common aspiration that pupils will learn, throughout their education, to become successful achievers, effective contributors and responsible citizens. Engaging pupils in decisions about their learning behaviour is clearly a potent medium for developing these qualities.

The intersubjective approach thus has enormous potential to establish collaborative working, restore learning, reduce classroom stress, and enhance relationships within the primary classroom, and represents a radical departure from a teacher-centred, managerial model. In some quarters, this way of working will pose a significant threat to current educational orthodoxy. Thus, whilst the framework set out in chapter six offers teachers the possibility of a practical alternative for dealing with chronic disengagement, we cannot overlook the possibility that certain individual, institutional and cultural barriers may constrain and subvert the intersubjective process. Since being aware of these barriers will better equip teachers to deal with them, let us consider each of the following in turn:

- teacher concerns about rights
- emotional intelligence
- school ethos and leadership
- educational policy and conditions of work

Teacher concerns about rights

There are two common concerns amongst teachers dealing with pupil disengagement that may undermine their sympathy for the idea of the intersubjective approach. The first is that addressing the needs of disengaging pupils in this way deprives other pupils of their right to an equitable share of teacher attention and finite resources. Thus the rights of the disengaging pupil are met at the expense of the rights of others. This argument is a major concern for teachers (GTC, 2005) and is not uncommonly used to justify the removal of disengagers from classrooms and schools.

The logic of this argument hinges on the underlying premise that all children should be treated the same and, on the surface at least, this seems perfectly reasonable and fair. It is a logic almost always raised in wider debates on discipline and inclusion, and it has a significant influence on public opinion on the matter.

This logic would be fine if all pupils were the same and had similar needs, but this is patently not the case. All pupils are different. Needs vary from pupil to pupil and will also vary considerably for every child over time, depending on the changing circumstances of home and school, shifts in personal relationships, health, etc. Thus, paradoxically, treating all pupils as if they were the same actually creates inequalities and injustice because it forces us to overlook diversity and to deny an individual's right to extra support when they need it. Such denials simply ensure that needs are not met and that disengagement and underachievement persist and thrive. A response like this is certainly not in anyone's interests, least of all the disengaging pupil's.

Although it is true that many teachers find it difficult to meet the range of needs that confront them in the primary classroom and that this may have an impact on other pupils, the problem does not lie with disengaging pupils or any other pupil in the classroom with additional support needs. Rather, it lies in school under-resourcing and issues of workload and class size (considered below). If these matters were resolved, teachers would be in a far better position to meet the needs of all their pupils and inclusion would become far more manageable. In this scenario all teachers and pupils would be winners.

The important point is that the rights argument does not stand up to scrutiny, and that pupils with additional support needs are not to blame for scarce resources in the primary school. Sadly, however, they are sometimes treated as though they are.

The second concern frequently raised by teachers is that meeting a pupil's right to participation in behavioural matters will translate into a right to do whatever they please, so is tantamount to 'giving in' or letting pupils 'get their own way'. The fear, once again, is that this preferential treatment may be achieved at the expense of teacher rights and the rights of other pupils who are happy to conform.

Underlying this argument is a fusion of two distinct ideas: the idea of pupil participation and the idea of loss of teacher control. They are united by a fear of the unknown, based on an understandable uncertainty about the consequences of opening up classroom decision-making to pupils after a long history of unilateral, teacher control. However, there is no logical necessity linking these two ideas together, and certainly no direct causal connection between them. Clearly everything hinges on what we mean by participation and how it operates in the classroom in practical terms.

It is perfectly possible for pupils to get their own way if teachers and parents allow them to. All it needs is for these adults to decide to entirely relinquish their own point of view and let pupils dominate. They would have to give away all their power. This is not what the intersubjective approach is about. On the contrary, this model is based on a three-way, triadic framework where the tendency for any one party to impose their point of view would inevitably be kept in check by the competing perspectives of the others. Thus, whilst pupils will certainly have had their say, so will their teachers and their parents. Far from having their own way, pupils will have to collaborate and negotiate a joint solution. This effectively ensures that power is shared.

Further, an intersubjective approach relies heavily on the leadership of the teacher who must have sufficient control to steer the process at all times. Clarifying boundaries and explaining what is and is not possible is part of the teacher's role: it is the teacher's job to uphold and protect the rights of all concerned. So if a pupil is getting everything their own way without the agreement of others, the teacher is not applying intersubjective principles faithfully.

But I must emphasise that teachers must be prepared to accept some loss of control over the content of the intersubjective process, such as decisions about what the behaviour means and how best to address it, since the specific aim is to share understanding and negotiate solutions. Teachers who cling to control will be unable to achieve this aim and will not be working intersubjectively either. Indeed, there is a chance that they will be getting their own way at the expense of pupils and parents. Some teachers may be more accepting of this outcome, but it simply takes us full circle, back to the imposed, managerial mode we have been trying to escape.

Teachers need to be aware of how their assumptions about rights might impact their judgement of the intersubjective model and sabotage the intersubjective process.

Emotional intelligence

Emotional intelligence is the capacity to recognise, understand and handle one's own emotions and those of other people (Faupel, 2006). Since the intersubjective process is itself an emotive one, likely to arouse participant feelings as well as deliberately focussing attention upon those linked to disengagement, it is obvious that emotional intelligence will have a bearing on its quality and effectiveness. Indeed, without a degree of emotional intelligence the intersubjective process will quickly falter.

The emotional intelligence of teachers is, then, fundamental to the success of the intersubjective approach, for it is underpinned by their capacity for reflective thought and action which, in turn, depends upon deeply personal qualities such as psychological maturity, patience, sensitivity, empathy. Qualities such as these vary from person to person. The intersubjective process will vary acccordingly, just as teaching varies according to individual differences.

Teachers therefore need to be emotionally intelligent. But this does not mean that they must be paragons of virtue in the primary classroom. What matters is that they can make a genuine attempt to actively listen to pupils and parents and to take their contributions seriously. It is the genuiness of the teacher's desire to help that lies at the heart of the intersubjective process, for pupils and parents always know when teachers are on their side – even in areas of disagreement. Thus, it is this willingness to stick by the pupil and the determination to support them through difficult times, that are the mark of the consummate, intersubjective practitioner. They are also a mark of emotional intelligence.

Equally, however, pupils and parents must play their part in the intersubjective process by ensuring that it remains an active and vital three-way collaboration. Their contribution, too, will be influenced by emotional intelligence. For example, pupils and parents may lack the interactive skills, confidence, or even the motivation to play a significant role in classroom decision-making. It is also possible that participants may have problems regulating their emotions. For example, some players in the triad may try to highjack the intersubjective process by using emotional blackmail to impose their will on others (Whitney, 1993). This can easily lead to hostility and conflict and to the problem of participants getting their own way.

The need for teachers to carefully anticipate and judge these matters was emphasised in the last chapter, and the importance of creating a supportive, structured and enabling context for intersubjectivity was highlighted. Teachers can also help considerably by creating a climate of emotional literacy in the primary classroom. This means noticing and acknowledging the emotions of all pupils. It entails explicitly helping pupils to recognise and understand emotions in themselves and others and to express their own feelings appropriately.

Nonetheless, despite a teacher's best efforts, a few pupils and parents may prefer to play a minimal role in the intersubjective process because of their poor emotional literacy. Occasionally, a pupil or parent may refuse the invitation outright, preferring that the teacher do this work for them. Or they may decide to abandon the process when they realise they will not get their own way entirely. Ultimately, there is little teachers can do in such situations, for one cannot coerce people into collaboration. It can only work with the combined good will and commitment of all parties.

However, if emotional literacy is modelled by the teacher, refusal, conflict and hostility are less likely. This means steadfastly upholding the governing principles of the intersubjective approach: sharing meanings, respecting diverse perspectives and negotiating solutions. Any slippage into a more didactic, controlling mode of interaction on the teacher's part will be counterproductive and send the wrong message. The solution, then, is to maintain an intersubjective orientation.

Ethos and leadership

The teacher's job will be made easier if the principles of intersubjectivity also permeate the wider school culture so that teachers feel supported in this way of working, and so that pupils and parents come to expect it. Though this may be something of an ideal, the point is an important one, for it directs us to the critical role of school ethos and leadership in matters of behaviour and discipline in the primary school.

It seems obvious that the work of teachers, pupils and parents experimenting with an intersubjective approach will be lightened if the institutional context is basically supportive of it, and will flourish if its core values of respect for the rights of others, for participation and justice, mirror those already guiding the habits, relationships, structures and way of life of the wider school. Clearly, we are not speaking of rhetorical values of the sort written into school policy documents or declaimed at important school gatherings, that have no real bearing on those lived throughout the school year. Many teachers will have worked in schools where this double think prevails and where a careful pre-sentation, or spin, is employed to convince outsiders of how important these values are to the institution. But pupils and parents are usually quick to see through such subterfuge, and will know the schools that cannot walk their talk.

What we are talking about is the 'emotionally literate primary school' (Colwell and Hammersley-Fletcher, 2005) – one in which rights and responsibilities are respected across the wider community, and where open communication and collaborative working are the *sine qua non* of everyday school life. This means headteachers, senior management teams, teaching and non-teaching staff, pupils and parents working together in a climate of trust and mutual respect. These values and practices directly inform the ethos of a school – its character and atmosphere and the quality of life possible within its walls. It is not difficult to identify a positive ethos when we come across it. We sense it the minute we enter a school and soon know that we are in a context that is person-centred, caring and ready to listen.

However, 'emotionally literate environments' require 'emotionally literate leadership' that can inspire 'empathy, engagement, respect... openness, honesty, transparency and trust' (Colwell and Hammersley-Fletcher, 2005, p3). These qualities are the building blocks of intersubjectivity, and will help teachers and pupils to establish the relationships central to effective collaboration. Emotional literacy therefore has a distinct bearing on the work of headteachers and management teams as well as teachers. Research suggests that emotionally literate leadership protects against teacher and pupil stress, promotes positive behaviour and enhances well-being (Dunlop *et al,* 2004; Colwell and Hammersley-Fletcher, 2005). Conversely, leadership that is remote, hierarchical and autocratic is likely to be unhelpful and alienating for everyone.

Teachers embarking on an intersubjective approach therefore need leaders who are emotionally literate. Such leaders are more likely to be convinced of the importance of investing in curriculi for social and emotional development such as PATHS (Promoting Alternative Thinking Strategies) (Greenberg *et al,* 1995) or SEAL (Social and Emotional Aspects of Learning) (DfES, 2005), and are more likely to encourage the uptake amongst staff of positive solution-focused approaches like the intersubjective approach, that prioritise prevention rather than reactivity and punishment.

Research suggests that schools with emotionally literate managers experience less poor behaviour (DfES, 2006; HMIE, 2005). However, this research is emphatic that the commitment of local authorities, school leaders *and* staff are all pivotal to success (*ibid*). Staff development at all levels therefore plays a decisive role in the creation of emotionally literate school environments. Training courses in this field are fast becoming a mainstay of initial teacher training and continuing professional development, and can help to build whole school capacity for positive relationships, partnership and empowerment.

This should, over time, enable more school leaders and teachers to deal positively and empathetically with pupils with challenging feelings and responses in the classroom, and should equip them with the basic skills and attitudes required for intersubjective teaching and learning. It should also help headteachers to respond sympathetically to teachers grappling with the stress of persistent disengagement and underachievement. It is crucial that these teachers feel able to ask for the support they need without fear of rejection, criticism or blame. This is a major concern for such teachers (GTC, 2005).

Educational policy and the conditions of work
It helps that current educational policy and legislation on social inclusion provides a broad rationale for an intersubjective approach to disengagement.

Participation lies at the very heart of the inclusive ideal. Policy and legislation ask us directly to listen to and involve pupils and parents in educational concerns, and gives teachers permission to adjust the curriculum and their teaching accordingly. Teachers need look no further for justification of the intersubjective approach. Intersubjectivity, it could be argued, is what makes inclusion happen. This trend in educational policy is highly encouraging and, providing a change of government does not bring it to a premature end, should give us hope that there is a future for the intersubjective model and the vision of collaborative practice associated with it.

Unfortunately, there is still much within educational culture that could undermine this vision of the future. For example, the standards agenda and the government obsession with teacher performance and accountability, normative testing and league tables, tends to lock schools and teachers into a preoccupation with outcomes that can dilute their focus on individual pupil needs and well-being. This obscures the moral purpose that lies at the very heart of teaching (Ball, 2005). It also tends to create a climate of competition within and between schools that has the potential to corrode the positive relationships essential to an inclusive ethos and to intersubjective practice.

We undoubtedly teach in difficult times. The standards agenda and the inclusion agenda seem to be opposing and mutually destructive forces. Teachers can understandably be overawed by this tension, and if we add to it the pressure of workload, the impact of class size, and an overkill of new initiatives, it is little wonder that many teachers currently retreat in confusion, seeking refuge in what is familiar and known, whilst a voluble minority express strong resistance to further innovation and change. Teachers in this mood may be resistant to the idea of intersubjectivity – who can blame them? But what happens, then, to pupils like Malcolm?

Teachers cannot afford to back away from this question, for teacher response to the circumstances of education has a direct influence on the lives disengaging pupils lead in school. So we cannot sit on the fence with impunity. If we say 'no' to change, we effectively say 'yes' to the *status quo*. This has direct consequences for teachers and pupils. Those who resist change must be sure that the *status quo* is what they really want.

It is also worth remembering that, whilst the current educational context is troubling and there is little practitioners can do to immediately transform their conditions of work for the better, it is ultimately individuals, not policy makers, who change things in schools. It is teachers, not policies, that pupils remember when they look back on school and recall those who have cared for and understood them. There is no reason why individual teachers cannot experiment with the intersubjective approach in order to find, like Mrs Parker in the Sommerville study, a realistic balance that works within the constraints of the current climate.

Good teachers have always done this: taken new ideas, made them their own, tried them out in their own classrooms and shared them with colleagues. In doing so, perhaps without realising it, teachers take control over their own professional development, influence educational practice from the bottom-up, and make a powerful statement about the nature of teacher professionalism. It is vital that teachers continue to explore and expand their practice in this time-honoured way, rather than waiting passively for the next batch of guidance to dictate to them. This response seems especially apposite in an educational context that purports to value teacher leadership, creativity and initiative. So we have an opportunity. Some would argue that it is a responsibility. Teachers must make their own decisions about whether they take it up.

Conclusion and implications

In the quote at the start of this chapter, Fielding (2001) articulates the view, increasingly expounded within educational circles, that teachers in the twenty first century must be prepared to dialogue with pupils, and should understand such encounters as central to professional learning. He is proposing that joint working should not be viewed as an 'add on' but as integral to the work of the teacher and as the basis for the development of teaching and learning.

If the inclusion agenda proves to be more than a passing fad, and the concern for standards can be kept in proportion, it is not unreasonable to expect that educational thinking will continue to shift in this direction to embrace a challenging new vision of teacher professionalism. This vision is based on the ideal of genuine inclusion and participation within what Bruner refers to as a 'viable pluralism' (Bruner, 1990, p30). This implies classrooms in which there is tolerance for the coexistence of multiple realities rather than insistence on conformity and uniformity, and willingness to engage with the messy, interactive human processes that underpin teaching and learning, rather than holding fast to more traditional, teacher-centred forms of practice.

This shift is important not just for disengaging pupils but for all pupils in primary school. It also has far wider implications – since the way we teach pupils and treat those who are excluded and alienated in classrooms today has an inescapable impact upon the generations of tomorrow. If our pupils are respected and listened to, they in turn will learn how to respect and listen to others, and will be able to contribute, as adults, to the creation of an inclusive society based on the principles of democratic participation and social justice. If this is the sort of society we want, then schools must prepare pupils for it but also, crucially, embody it (Bruner, 1996).

In his classic text, *On Dialogue*, Bohm (1996) sets out a vision of society based on such principles. He argues passionately that if shared understanding were slowly to permeate our culture, it would foster confidence and well-being and act like 'glue' bringing strength and coherence to interpersonal relationships at all levels of society. He asserts:

> '...shared meaning is really the cement that holds society together, and you could say that the present society has very poor cement. If you make a building with very low quality cement, it cracks and falls apart. We really need the right cement, the right glue. And that is shared meaning.' (Bohm, 1996, p29)

Mrs Parker and other teachers like her appear to have found the glue that Bohm is speaking of. The 'Mrs Parkers' of the primary classroom are in the vanguard of this new vision. Yet, for the moment, this is the path less travelled in the primary school. If, as the findings of this book suggest, the path is worth exploring further, then future research must focus on how the profession can continue to build upon intersubjective principles and establish the foundations of a classroom culture based not on conformity to cultural norms and silent acquiescence but on a respect for individual differences; a culture in which pupils, teachers and parents can be sure of a 'fair hearing' (John, 1996).

Not so long ago, this notion of intersubjectivity would have been considered impossibly naïve and hopelessly idealistic. Perhaps now this idea has finally found its time. I hope that this book might make a small contribution towards its realisation by helping teachers begin the process of making sense of disengagement *alongside* pupils and parents.

***

A final message from pupils...

Disengaging pupils in the primary years do not generally reject learning *per se*. What they reject is learning that is dull, imposed, disconnected from their interests and concerns and poorly matched to their learning styles and needs. They also reject teachers who do not listen to them or try to understand them. Yet disengaging pupils acknowledge that their problems do not lie just with teachers and schools. They know that their own feelings, attitudes and habits get in the way of their learning, and that personal and family concerns impinge on their responses in the classroom.

On the whole, theses pupils do not pretend that their behaviour is unproblematic. They acknowledge that mucking around, chatting, daydreaming and disturbing others invariably undermines their progress and inevitably leads to conflicts with teachers and parents. Though disengagement is fun, they realise that it comes at a high price. This worries many of these pupils. They would like things to change, but many of them resist the idea that they alone should do all the changing. Teachers and schools need to change as well. Above all, teachers need to listen and try to understand.

Are we listening?

References

Alderson, P. (2004) Ethics in Fraser, S., Lewis,V., Ding, S., Kellett, M. and Robinson, C. (eds) *Doing Research with Children and Young People*, London: Sage, 97-112

Araujo, M. (2005) Disruptive or Disrupted? a qualitative study on the construction of in-discipline, *International Journal of Inclusive Education*, 9/3, 241-268

Ball, S. (2004) Education Reform as Social Barbarism: economism and the end of authenticity, *Scottish Educational Review*, 37/1, 4-16

Baxter, J. (1999) Screening for Mental Health Problems in Young Children: can we expect teachers to get it right? *Young Minds*, 42, 12-14

Blatchford, P. (2003) *The Class Size Debate: is small better?* Maidenhead: Open University Press

Blatchford, P. and Martin, C. (1998) The Effects of Class Size on Classroom Processes: it's a bit like a treadmill – working hard and getting nowhere fast! *British Journal of Educational Studies* 46/2 p118-137

Blease, D. (1995) Teachers' Judgments of Their Pupils: broad categories and multiple criteria, *Educational Studies* 21/2 p203-215

Bohm, D. (1996) *On Dialogue*, London: Routledge

Brown, S. and McIntyre, D. (1993) *Making Sense of Teaching*, Buckingham: Open University Press

Bruner, J. (1990) *Acts of Meaning*, London: Harvard University Press

Bruner, J. (1996) *The Culture of Education*, London: Harvard University Press

Butt, R., Raymond, D., McCue, G. and Yamagishi, L. (1992) Collaborative Autobiography and the Teacher's Voice, in Goodson, I. F. (ed) *Studying Teachers' Lives*, London: Routledge

Carr, W. and Kemmis, S. (1986) *Becoming Critical: knowing through action research*, London: Falmer

Charlton, T. and David, K. (1993) (eds) *Managing Misbehaviour in Schools*, London: Routledge

Cohen, A.P. (1994) *Self-Consciousness: an alternative anthropology of identity*, London: Routledge

Colwell, H. and Hammersley-Fletcher, L. (2005) The Emotionally Literate Primary School Available: www.staffs.ac.uk/schools/business/iepr/docs/Working-paper15.doc

Cooley, A.P. (1902) *Human Nature and the Social Order*, New York: Charles Scribner and Sons

Cooper, P. (1993a) Learning from Pupil Perspectives, *British Journal of Special Education*, 20/4, 129-133

Cooper, P. (1993b) Field Relations and the Problem of Authenticity: researching participant's perceptions of teaching and learning in classrooms, *British Educational Research Journal*, 19/4, 323-338

Cooper, P. (2006) Setting the Scene, in Hunter-Carsch, M., Tiknas, Y., Cooper, P. and Sage, R. (eds) *The Handbook of Social Emotional and Behavioural Dificulties*, London: Continuum.

Crozier, J. (1999) Is it a Case of 'We know when we're not wanted'? the parents' perspective on parent-teacher roles and relationships, *Educational Research*, 41/3, 315-328

Crozier, G. and Reay, D. (Eds) (2005) *Activating Participation: parents and teachers working towards partnership*, Stoke on Trent: Trentham

Cullingford, C. (1985) The Idea of the School: the expectations of parents, teachers and children, in Cullingford, C. (ed) *Parents, Teachers and Schools*, London: Boyce

Cullingford, C. and Morrison, M. (1999) Relationships between Parents and Schools: a case study, *Educational Review*, 51/3, 254-262

Davies, B. (1980) An Analysis of Primary School Children's Accounts of Classroom Interaction, *British Journal of Sociology of Education* 1/3, 257-275

Dewe, P. J. (1985) Coping with Stress: an investigation of teachers' actions, *Research in Education*, 33, 27-40

Dewey, J. (1933) *How We Think: a restatement of the relation of reflective thinking to the educative process*, Chicago: Henry Regnery

DfEE (2001) *Continuing Professional Development*, Nottingham: DfEE

DfES (2003b) *Every Child Matters: Green Paper*, London: Stationary Office

DfES (2003d) *Fast-track Competencies and Values* Available: www.fasttrackteaching.gov.uk

DfES (2005) *Social and Emotional Aspects of Learning: improving learning, improving behaviour*, Nottingham: DFES

DfES (2006) *Evaluation of the Primary Behaviour and Attendance Pilot*, Nottingham: DfES

Donaldson, M. (1978) *Children's Minds*, London: Penguin

Donaldson, M. (1992) *Human Minds*, London: Penguin

Dunlop, C.A. and Macdonald, E. B. (2004) *The Teachers Health and Wellbeing Study Scotland*, Edinburgh: NHS Health Scotland

Elliott, J. (1991) *Action Research for Educational Change*, Buckingham: Open University Press

Facer, K., Furlong, J., Furlong, R. and Sutherland, R. (2003) 'Edutainment' Software: a site for cultures in conflict, in Sutherland, R, Claxton, G. and Pollard, A. (eds) *Learning and Teaching where Worldviews Meet*, Stoke on Trent: Trentham, 207-225

Faupel, A. (2006) Promoting Emotional Literacy: its implications for school and classroom practice, in Hunter-Carsch. M., Tiknaz, Y., Cooper, P. and Sage, R. (eds) *The Handbook of Social Emotional and Behavioural Difficulties*, London: Continuum, 167-175

Fielding, M. (2001) Students as Radical Agents of Change, *Journal of Educational Change*, 2, 123-141

Fielding, M. (2004) Transformative Approaches to Student Voice: theoretical underpinnings and recalcitrant realities, *British Educational Research Journal*, 30/2, 295-311

Fielding, M. and Rudduck, J. (2002) *The Transformative Potential of Student Voice: confronting the power issues*, presented at the Conference of the British Educational Research Association, University Of Exeter

Flouri, E. and Buchanan, A. (2004) Early Father's and Mother's Involvement and Child's Later Educational Outcome, *British Educational Psychology*, 74, 141-153

Flutter, J. and Rudduck, J. (2004) *Consulting Pupils: what's in it for schools?* London: Routledge

Fullan, M. (1991) *The New Meaning of Educational Change*, New York: Teachers' College Press

Gardner, H. (1993) *Frames of Mind: the theory of multiple intelligences*, London: Fontana

Goleman, D. (1996) *Emotional Intelligence*, London: Bloomsbury

Goleman, D. (1997) *Vital Lies, Simple Truths: the psychology of self-deception*, London: Bloomsbury

Goodnow, J. and Burns, A. (1991) Teachers: a child's eye view, in Woodhead, M., Light, P. and Carr, R. (eds) *Growing up in a Changing Society*, London: Open University Press

Goodson, I. (1992) (ed) *Studying Teachers' Lives*, London: Routledge

Greenburg, M., Kusche, C., Cooke, E. and Quamma, J. (1995) Promoting Emotional Competence in School-Aged Children – The Effects of the PATHS Curriculum, *Development and Psychopathology*, 7/1, 179-136

GTC (General Teaching Council Scotland) (2005) *Discipline in Scottish Schools: a survey of teacher's views*, Edinburgh: GTC

Hanko, G. (1994) Discouraged Children: when praise does not help, *British Journal of Special Education*, 21/4, 166-168

Hanko, G. (2003) Towards an Inclusive School Culture – but what happened to Elton's affective curriculum?, *British Journal of Special Education*, 30/3, 125-131

Hargreaves, A. (1994) *Changing Teachers: Changing Times*, London: Cassell

Head, G. (2003) Effective Collaboration: deep collaboration as an essential element of the learning process, *Journal of Educational Enquiry*, 4/2, 47-62

Hinett, K. (2003) *Improving Learning through Reflection – Part 1* Available: www.ilt.ac.uk

HMI (2005) *Parents' Satisfaction with Schools* Available at www.ofsted.gov.uk

HMIE (HM Inspectorate of Education) (2005) *A Climate for Learning: a review of the implementation of the Better Behaviour – Better Learning report* Available: www.hmie.gov.uk

Hughes, M. and Greenhough, P. (2003) Homework: learning at the interface between home and school cultures, in Sutherland, R., Claxton, G. and Pollard, A. (eds) *Learning and Teaching where Worldviews Meet*, Stoke on Trent: Trentham, 179-192

Hyman, I. (1990) Class-Cutting: an ecological approach, in Gupta, R. M. and Coxhead, P. (eds) *Intervention with Children*, London: Routledge

Jackson, M. (1987) Making Sense of School, in A. Pollard (ed) *Children and their Primary Schools*, London: Falmer

James, A., Jenks, C. and Prout, A. (1998) *Theorizing Childhood*, Cambridge: Polity Press

John, M. (1996) *Children in Charge: the child's right to a fair hearing*, London: Jessica Kingsley

Jones, K. and Lock, M. (1993) Working with Parents, in Charlton, T. and David, K. (eds) *Managing Misbehaviour*, London: Routledge

Keys, W., Harris, S. and Fernandes, C. (1995) *Attitudes to School of Top Primary and First Year Secondary Pupils*, Slough: NFER

Laird, R. D., Jordan, K.V., Dodge, K.A. and Bates, J.E. (2001) Peer Rejection in Childhood, Involvement with Antisocial Peers in Early Adolescence and Development of Externalising Behaviour Problems, *Development Psychopathology,* 13, 337-354

Lee, N. (2001) *Childhood and Society,* Buckingham: Open University Press

Lindsay, G. (2000) Researching Children's Perspectives: ethical issues, in A. Lewis and G. Lindsay (eds) *Researching Children's Perspectives,* Buckingham: Open University Press, 3-20

Maclure, M. (1993) Arguing for Your Self: identity as an organising principle in teacher's jobs and lives, *British Educational Research Journal,* 19/4, 311-32

Maclure, M. and Walker, B. M. (2000) Disenchanted Evenings: the social organisation of talk in parent-teacher consultations, *British Journal of Sociology of Education,* 21/1, 5-24

Macrae, S., Maguire, M. and Milbourne, L. (2003) Social Exclusion: exclusion from school, *International Journal of Inclusive Education,* 7/2, 89-101

McFadden M and Munns G (2002) Student Engagement and the Social Relations of Pedagogy, *British Journal of Sociology of Education,* 23/3

McManus, M. (1995) *Troublesome Children in the Classroom,* London: Routledge

Meighan, R. (1989) The Parents and the Schools: alternative role definitions, *Educational Review,* 41/2, 105-112

Merrett, F. and Jones, L. (1994) Rules, Sanctions and Rewards in Primary Schools, *Educational Studies,* 20/3, 345-355

Munn, P., Johnstone, M. and Chalmers, V. (1992) *Effective Discipline in Primary Schools and Classrooms,* London: Chapman

Munn, P., Johnstone, M., and Sharp, S. (2004) *Teacher's Perceptions of Discipline in Schools,* Edinburgh: Scottish Executive Education Department Available: http//www.Scotland.gov.uk

Pollard, A. (1985) *The Social World of the Primary School,* London: Holt

Pollard, A. (1987) *Children and their Primary Schools,* London: Falmer

Pollard, A. (2005) (2nd edition) *Reflective Teaching,* London: Continuum

Pollard, A. and Filer, A. (2003) Parental Strategies at the Intersection of Home and School Cultures: the mediation of formal assessment, in Sutherland, R., Claxton, G. and Pollard, A. (eds) *Learning and Teaching where Worldviews Meet,* Stoke on Trent: Trentham, 193-206

Pollard, A. and Tann, S. (1987) *Reflective Teaching in the Primary School: a handbook for the classroom,* London: Cassell

Pollard, A. and Triggs, P. (2000) *What Pupils Say: changing policy and practice in primary education,* London: Continuum

QAA (Quality Assurance Agency) (2000) *Standard for Initial Teacher Education in Scotland* Available: www.qaa.ac.uk

Qvortrup, J. (1990) A Voice for Children in Statistical and Social Accounting: a plea for children's right to be heard, in James, A. and Prout, A. (eds) *Constructing and Reconstructing Childhood,* London: Falmer

Reynolds, D. and Cuttance, P. (1992) *School Effectiveness: research, policy and practice,* London: Cassell

Riley, K.A. and Docking, J. (2004) Voices of Disaffected Pupils: implications for policy and practice, *British Journal of Educational Studies,* 52/2,166-179

Riley, K.A. and Rustique-Forrester, E. (2002) *Working with Disaffected Students: why students lose interest in schools and what we can do about it,* London: Paul Chapman

Rogers, C. (1969) *Freedom to Learn*, London: Charles E. Merill

Russell, K. and Granville, S. (2005) *Parents' Views on Improving Parental Involvement in Children's Education*, Edinburgh: Scottish Executive

Schon, D. A. (1983) *The Reflective Practitioner: how professionals think in action*, London: Temple Smith

Schostak, J. F. and Logan, T. (1984) *Pupil Experience*, London: Croom Helm

SEED (Scottish Executive Education Department) (2001) *Better Behaviour-Better Learning: summary report of the discipline task group*, Edinburgh: SEED

SEED (2002) *Chartered Teacher Programme for Scotland* Available. www.scotland.gov.uk

SEED (2004a) *A Curriculum for Excellence: The Curriculum Review Group*, Edinburgh: Scottish Executive

SEED (2005) *Scottish Schools (Parental Involvement) Bill – Policy Memorandum*, Edinburgh: SEED

Sherman, A. (1997) Five-Year-Olds' Perceptions of Why We Go to School, *Children and Society* 2/2, 117-127

Silcock, P. (1994) The Process of Reflective Teaching, *British Journal of Education Studies*, 42/3, 273-285

Sinclair Taylor, A. (2000) The UN Convention on the Rights of the Child: giving children a voice in Lewis, A. and Lindsay, G. (eds) *Researching Children's Perspectives*, Buckingham: Open University Press

Slee, R. (1995) *Changing Theories and Practices of Discipline*, London: Falmer

Soloman, Y and Rogers, C. (2001) Motivational Patterns in Disaffected School Students: insights from pupil referral units, *British Educational Research Journal*, 27/3, 331-345

Somekh, B. (1994) Inhabiting Each Other's Castles: towards knowledge and mutual growth through collaboration, *Action Research*, 2/3, 357-376

Somekh, B. (2006) *Action Research: a methodology for change and development*, Buckingham: Open University

Tett, L., Cadell, D., Crowther, J. and O'Hara, P. (2001) Parents and Schools: partnerships in early primary education, *Scottish Educational Review*, 33/1, 48-58

Tizard, B. and Hughes, M. (1984) *Young Children Learning: talking and thinking at home and at school*, London: Fontana

Todd, L. (2003) Disability and the Restructuring of Welfare: the problem of partnership with parents, *International Journal of Inclusive Education*, 7/3, 281-296

Todd, S. and Higgins, S. (1998) Powerlessness in Professional and Parent Partnerships, *British Journal of Sociology of Education*, 19/2, 227-236

Tomlinson, J. (1997) Values: the curriculum of moral education, *Children and Society*, 11/4, 242-252

Trowell, J. and Bower, M. (1995) *The Emotional Needs of Children and their Families*, London: Routledge

Upton, G. (1993) Understanding Interaction: the dynamics of emotional and behavioural difficulties, in Charlton, T. and David, K. (eds) *Managing Misbehaviour in Schools*, London: Routledge

Usher, R. and Edwards, R. (1994) *Postmodernism and Education*, London: Routledge

Van Manen, M. (1997 2nd edn) *Researching Lived Experience*, Ontario: Althouse Press

Vincent, C. (1996) *Parents and Teachers: power and participation*, London: Falmer

Vincent, C. and Martin, J. (2005) Parents as Citizens: making the case in: G. Crozier and D. Reay (eds) *Activating Participation: parents and teachers working towards partnership*, Stoke on Trent: Trentham

Watkins, C. and Wagner, P. (2000) *Improving School Behaviour*, London: Paul Chapman

Weare, K. and Gray, G. (2003) *What Works in Developing Children's Emotional and Social Competence and Wellbeing?* London: DfES

Wells, J., Barlow, J, and Stewart-Brown, S. (2003) A Systematic Review of Universal Approaches to Mental Health Promotion in Schools, *Health Education*, 4, 197-220

Whitney, B. (1993) *The Children Act and Schools*, London: Kogan Page

Wilson, N. (1991) *With the Best of Intentions*, Nairne, South Australia, Wilson

Wing, L. A. (1995) Play is not the Work of the Child: young children's perceptions of work and play, *Early Childhood Research Quarterly*, 10, 223-247

Woods, P., Jeffrey, B., Troman, G. and Boyle, M. (1997) *Restructuring Schools, Restructuring Teachers: responding to change in the primary school*, Buckingham: Open University Press

Zay, D. (1999) Thinking the Interactive Interplay between Reflection/Practice/Partnership: questions and points of tension, *Pedagogy, Culture and Society*, 7/2, 195-219

Index